A
NEW EARTH
Methods, Exercises, Formulas and Prayers

Translated from the French
Original title : LA NOUVELLE TERRE
Méthodes, exercices, formules, prières

Omraam Mikhaël Aïvanhov

A
NEW EARTH
Methods, Exercises, Formulas and Prayers

5th Edition

Translated from the French

Complete Works — Volume 13

P R O S V E T A

Prosveta S.A. — B.P. 12 — 83601 Fréjus Cedex (France)

ISBN 2-85566-622-8
édition originale : PROSVETA SUISSE 1975

TABLE OF CONTENTS

Foreword

It will help you to understand my role as a teacher and educator if I compare myself to a rich man who invites many friends to a banquet. I want to be sure that all my guests have what they need, so I put before them a great variety of dishes—every kind of fruit, vegetable, cheese, and so on—so that each one may choose what suits him or her best. No one is obliged to sample every dish on the table. In fact, if they were to do so they would only make themselves ill.

And this applies to my teaching as well: I put a wide variety of methods before you, because I know that the needs of each one of you are different. Your characters, faculties, and capacity for work are all different, and only you can decide which method suits you best. You must not try to apply them all. It would be dangerous to do so. Of course, you should keep in mind the numerous rules I have given you for your daily lives, for they will keep you from going astray and help to further your evolution. But you must not attempt to do every exercise or apply all the methods I have recommended. You would only give yourself a nervous breakdown. Be warned therefore: you are guests at a banquet; the table is laden with every imaginable variety of food, and you must be selective and not try to eat everything. Concentrate on just a few methods—four or five, six or seven—and use them for a work in depth.

And now I should add something that is very important from a psychological point of view. You will sometimes find that a method that gave you great light, consolation, and courage yesterday is powerless to help you today, because you are not in the same mood or your circumstances have changed. What should you do? Do not insist. Simply try to find another method that will help you today. Here too you can draw the comparison with food. There are days when you feel like eating an omelette or some pasta, and others when you would much rather have fish, or cheese, or just fruit. And this is as it should be, for our bodies need a variety of foods. It is not good to eat always the same thing. Of course, I know that there are communities in which the people eat the same thing every day, but a restricted diet of this kind is the result of special conditions, and these people have been accustomed to it for hundreds of years. In any case, it is up to each one of you to sense whether or not a method that helped you yesterday is what you need today, and, if not, to put it aside for the time being. You can always go back to it another day.

Cosmic intelligence wishes human beings to develop their full potential and achieve fulfilment. This is why you must not be content to do the same thing every day. If you want to advance you must continually experiment and discover new methods. Consider all the different acts you perform in a day. At different moments, depending on circumstances, you use your brain, your eyes or ears, your arms or legs, and in doing so you learn and make progress. Your physical organs and members are always there and always the same, but you do not use them all at the same time. You use them at different times, depending on your needs and circumstances. And you should apply the same principle to the way you use the methods I give you. Learn to use them wisely, according to your needs.

Omraam Mikhaël Aïvanhov

Chapter One

Prayers

In certain circumstances, the following prayers are recited in common.

The Lord's Prayer

Our Father, who art in heaven, hallowed be thy name.
Thy kingdom come, thy will be done
On earth as it is in heaven.
Give us this day our daily bread.
And forgive us our trespasses
As we forgive those who trespass against us.
And lead us not into temptation
    But deliver us from evil.
For thine is the kingdom, the power and the glory
For ever and ever. Amen.

The Good Prayer

Lord God, sweet heavenly Father, who has given us life and health so that we may worship you with joy, send your spirit to protect us and keep us from evil thoughts and from all harm.

Teach us to do your will, to bless your name, to glorify you without ceasing.

Sanctify our spirits, and uplift our hearts and minds so that we may keep your commandments and laws.

Inspire pure thoughts in us by your sacred presence and guide us so that we may serve you joyfully.

Bless our lives which we consecrate to you for the greater good of our brothers and sisters and all who are dear to us.

Help and assist us so that we may grow every day in wisdom and understanding, and live always in your truth.

Guide us in all our undertakings so that everything we do for your holy name may contribute to the coming of your kingdom on earth.

Nourish our souls with bread from heaven and give us your strength in abundance so that our lives may be successful.

And as you lavish all blessings on us, grant us also the gift of your love, so that it may ever be our law.

For thine is the kingdom, the power and the glory, for ever and ever. Amen.

Psalm 91

He who dwells in the secret place of the Most High
Shall abide under the shadow of the Almighty.
I will say of the Lord: 'He is my refuge and my fortress;
My God, in him I will trust.'
Surely he shall deliver you from the snare of the fowler
And from the perilous pestilence.
He shall cover you with his feathers,
And under his wings you shall take refuge;
His truth shall be your shield and buckler.
You shall not be afraid of the terror by night,
Nor of the arrow that flies by day,
Nor of the pestilence that walks in darkness,
Nor of the destruction that lays waste at noonday.
A thousand may fall at your side,
And ten thousand at your right hand;
But it shall not come near you.
Only with your eyes shall you look,
And see the reward of the wicked.
Because you have made of the Lord, who is my refuge,
Even the Most High, your habitation,
No evil shall befall you,
Nor shall any plague come near your dwelling;
For he shall give his angels charge over you,
To keep you in all your ways.
They shall bear you up in their hands,
Lest you dash your foot against a stone.
You shall tread upon the lion and the cobra,
The young lion and the serpent you shall trample underfoot.
Because he has set his love upon me, therefore
I will deliver him;
I will set him on high, because he has known my name.
He shall call upon me, and I will answer him;

I will be with him in trouble;
I will deliver him and honour him.
With long life I will satisfy him,
And show him my salvation.

Chapter Two

A Daily Programme[1]

1.The purpose of this chapter is not to suggest a detailed programme for the day. It simply enumerates the highlights of an average day, with the relevant exercises and methods indicated by the Master Omraam Michaël Aïvanhov, as well as some general recommendations for our daily lives.

Omraam Mikhaël Aïvanhov

Morning

Prayer on awakening

When you wake up in the morning, the very first thing you must do, before anything else, is to give thanks to the Lord. The first words to pass your lips should be: 'Thank you, Lord, for giving me life and health. Fill my heart with love, and give me the strength to do your will so that all my actions may be in your name and for your glory.'

Remembering your dreams

As soon as you have expressed your gratitude to heaven, you should try to remember your dreams. If you get into the habit of doing this, you will often find that while you were asleep you have been given a programme for the day ahead. But you have to do this at once, while the images of your dream are still vivid; if you delay you will very rarely be able to recall anything. Sometimes our dreams come back to us in the course of the day, but it is better to try and remember them when we wake up in the morning.

Getting out of bed

The next thing to do is to get up. If you are in the habit of lying in bed after you wake up, you are exposing yourself to considerable danger on the psychic plane: you will be tempted to linger in a twilight state, drifting in an astral fantasy world of sloth and sensuality which will sap your will-power and destroy your character, and you will be permanently crippled. The habit will make a sluggard of you, a prisoner of your imagination, bent on the pursuit of pleasure.

You must get out of bed forwards, never backwards, and put your right foot to the ground first. Details like this may seem unimportant but, in fact, each one is significant: each movement when you are getting up in the morning should be made consciously and correctly.

Morning ablutions

Once you are up, the first thing to do is to wash. Before praying, before doing anything else, wash your hands and face, and be particularly careful not to touch your eyes before you have washed your hands.

The Cabbalah tells us that at night, when we are asleep, an unclean spirit attaches itself to our physical body. In the morning, when you wake, that spirit is still there; your hands and face are still under its influence. Before you do anything else, therefore, you must rid yourself of the fluidic layer of impurities still clinging to your hands and face.

Wash yourself consciously and carefully, for washing is just as important as eating, and you must be careful not to do it hurriedly or roughly. This is particularly important when you are washing your face, for the particles of the etheric body are arranged in such subtle order that rough, clumsy gestures can seriously disturb them. Observe yourself when you wash, and you will see that if you are careless and in a hurry you demagnetize yourself.

While you are washing, concentrate on the refreshing effect of the water on your skin, for this sensation will help to clarify your thoughts. Try to feel the sacredness of what you are doing, and say, 'May my face shine with God's love,' or, 'As I wash my physical face, so may my spiritual face be washed.' Or still, 'In the name of immortal, everlasting love, in the name of immortal, everlasting wisdom, in which we live and have our being, may this water deliver me from all impurities.' And spend a few moments in prayer.

A cup of hot water

A cup of well boiled, piping hot water every morning on an empty stomach is an excellent way of cleansing your organism. Hot water is a perfectly harmless and very potent, natural remedy. Certain deposits in our bodies can only be eliminated by fasting or drinking very hot water, for the heat dilates the tissues and improves the circulation. Try it, and you will see how many complaints can be avoided or cured by the regular use of hot water: migraine, fever, loss of appetite, insomnia, etc. Arteriosclerosis is a hardening of the walls of the arteries caused by the accumulation of certain substances. Hot water can dissolve many of these deposits and restore elasticity to the arterial tissue.

Meditation[1]

Before embarking on the activities of the day, you should sit down quietly and allow peace to flood into you; establish a harmonious contact with the whole universe and with God your creator, and, by prayer and meditation, consecrate your day to him.

1.The teaching of the Universal White Brotherhood recommends that from 21 March to 21 September the disciples attend the sunrise every morning. See chaps. 9 and 10 for further explanations and methods of meditation.

Here is an exercise you can do every morning:

Raise your right arm, your hand outstretched, and imagine that you are projecting your astral hand up to the very throne of God. Then say: 'My God, all I have is yours; make use of me for the triumph and glory of your kingdom. I promise to do your will. May your love, wisdom, and power manifest themselves through me.' There will be days when you are incapable of repeating this formula wholeheartedly; you sense that there is something in you that refuses to give way. You must try to reach the point of being able to say these words in all sincerity, not just from time to time, but every day.

Blessed are those who can say, 'My God, I am your servant; do what you will with me.'

Breathing exercises

Breathing is a form of nutrition, and just as we have to chew our food thoroughly, in the same way, when we breathe, we should 'chew' the air. When you breathe in you should hold the air in your lungs (which are a kind of stomach) until they have had time to assimilate fully all the nutritional substances it contains. If you expel the air from your lungs almost at once, you reject these substances before your organism has had time to extract the beneficial elements.

Description of the breathing exercises:

1. Begin by closing your left nostril and breathing in deeply through the right nostril, to the count of 4.

2. Hold your breath to the count of 16.

3. Close your right nostril and breathe out through the left nostril to the count of 8.

4. Still with the right nostril closed, breathe in through the left nostril to the count of 4.

5. Hold your breath to the count of 16.

6. Breathe out through the right nostril to the count of 8.

Repeat these six steps six times in all. If you are capable of doing so, you can double the time of each movement, counting 8, 32, 16.

Deep breathing can be extremely efficacious in healing your nervous system and treating many other disorders. If you have a deficiency of calcium, sodium, iodine, etc., a doctor would prescribe a series of injections, whereas an initiate would begin by advising the absorption of these elements on the etheric plane by means of breathing exercises. The way to do this is extremely simple: while breathing, you concentrate on the idea that you are taking from the air whatever element is lacking. Yes, your body is well aware of what it needs; it has its own team of very efficient chemists who are able to extract the substances you need from the air you breathe. This is why disciples can never be content with the medicines sold in the chemist's shop. They prefer to breathe with love, knowing that they can draw the elements they need from the atmosphere.

But this is not all: you can also draw into yourself substances, forces, and particles from the world above, such as light, peace, and an abundance of life-giving elements. When you breathe, therefore, you should seek to draw into yourself the spiritual elements that you most need at the time.

Mental exercises to accompany deep breathing

1. Choose four virtues that you are particularly anxious to develop: while breathing in to the count of 4, say the names of these four virtues mentally.

While holding your breath to the count of 16, repeat the four names four times.

As you breathe out, say to yourself: 'I expel all...' and mention the four faults or vices that are the opposite of the four virtues you have chosen.

2. While breathing in, say inwardly: 'Thank you, Lord, for allowing me to breathe this pure air and the divine life with which you have filled it.'
While holding your breath: 'May this divine life penetrate my whole body and give it life and health.'
While breathing out: 'I shall manifest this life I have received through all my actions, for the glory of God.'
3. While breathing in: 'My God, may your name be blessed in me.'
While holding your breath: 'My God, may your kingdom and your righteousness be established in me.'
While breathing out: 'My God, may your will be done in me.'
4. While breathing in, repeat the names of four virtues twice.
While breathing out, think of the angels of the four elements who are working to rid you of all impurities: the angel of fire in your brain; the angel of air in your lungs and heart; the angel of water in your stomach, intestines, and sexual organs; and the angel of carth in your whole body.

Meals[2]

Before and after each meal, the disciples of the Universal White Brotherhood recite the following formula in Bulgarian, three times: *Bojiata lubov razreshava vsickite problemi.* (The love of God resolves all problems).

General Recommendations

Living each day to the full

Your entire destiny is contained in and determined by the way you live today: the orientation you give to your thoughts

2.See chap. 3 for detailed explanations of how to eat.

and feelings, and the activities on which you choose to spend your energies. The quality of your life and the care and vigilance you bring to it today determine whether the future will be an open path before you, or whether, on the contrary, it will be cluttered with all kinds of useless and even harmful things which will impede your development.

This is what Jesus meant when he told his disciples not to worry about tomorrow, for if you are careful to do everything exactly as it should be done every single day, then each successive day will be free of impediments, and although you will always have to take care not to leave loose ends lying about, there will be nothing to prevent you from undertaking whatever you please. In this way, each new day will find you fresh and ready to breathe and study, sing and enjoy whatever comes; your whole life will be coloured by gladness and blessedness. This is what you must understand. You prepare the morrow by taking care to do everything correctly today.

So do not think about tomorrow; think about today. If everything goes well today, everything will go well tomorrow also—it is automatic. And since every single event goes down on record, when you live one splendid, eternal day, it is recorded. It can never die or disappear; it remains forever alive, a beacon and example to those that follow. Try to live just one perfect day, for it will influence all those that come after it; it will call a meeting with them to discuss their behaviour, and then it will persuade them to be as well balanced, orderly, and harmonious as itself.

As you have never studied the magical aspect, you think, 'Oh, just one day—what difference can it make? I know that today wasn't too good, but tomorrow will be better.' Will it? It all depends. It can be if you try immediately to restore order. Otherwise it will be like a game of skittles: each day that falls knocks over the next one, and then another and another.

Constant vigilance

Often enough, if you ask people what they are thinking, they will reply that they do not know. They have never learned to observe themselves, so they have no idea of the currents that pass through them, of all the filth and horror that goes on in their minds. In these conditions, how can their work be built on a firm foundation?

The Bible tells us to be sober and vigilant, 'Because your adversary, the devil, walks about like a roaring lion, seeking whom he may devour.' Of course, you will not see any lions or devils in the physical dimension; it is in your inner life that you are in danger. It is on this level that all kinds of desires, passions, and lusts conspire to annihilate you, and if you are not enlightened and very vigilant you can bring disaster on yourself.

It is not enough simply to avoid falling and hurting oneself or breaking something on the physical level; you also have to take care not to break the laws of the invisible world. Without knowing it, you can trigger certain mechanisms, disturb certain entities, or break a law on the psychic level, and then you have to accept the consequences: you will be punished.

The most important thing for a disciple to understand, therefore, is that he must keep an eye on what goes on within himself; he must be constantly watchful and fully conscious and capable of discerning at each instant the true nature of the currents, desires, thoughts, influences, and impulses to which he is subject. By cultivating this total awareness and continuing to nourish a high ideal, he puts himself in the company of entities and intelligences of a higher order, and one day these sublime beings will dwell in him and enable him to assume great responsibilities and overcome numerous difficulties.

Directing one's energies

In the great book of living nature, it is written that it is of the utmost importance for the evolution of each human being that they should be able to account for the energy they spend and know exactly how and for what purpose they use it. They have been given a certain sum of energy which has been carefully counted, weighed, and measured, and they are responsible for it. Heaven has not given it to them so that they can waste it; everything they do is noted and put on record. In the book of living nature, therefore, you can find these words: 'Blessed are those who dedicate and employ all their physical, emotional, and mental energies for the good of mankind and for the kingdom of God and his righteousness.'

If you squander your energies in fits of rage, sensual excesses, and criminal or purely selfish activities, they will fuel the fires of hell; it is the ignorance of human beings that continues to nourish and sustain hell. Human beings are extremely knowledgeable in scientific matters, but they have never even heard or thought of their responsibility in regard to the use they make of their energies.

One of the first tasks of a disciple is to examine his goals and see whether he is using his energies for purely selfish motives or whether his goal is divine. This is what matters. If you asked yourself this question every day, you would find a great many aspects of your lives that could be tremendously improved. Of course, you cannot expect to make everything perfect all at once, but at least it would teach you to be conscious of what is going on. Never forget that if you do not do this, you will continue to be subject to your karma, to destiny.

In all that I tell you, you must pick out the things that you should think about every day and those that you must think about in certain specific circumstances. A great many of the things I tell you can be left to one side, but not this. This is something that has to be done every day: be conscious and aware at each instant of how you are using your energies. It is very easy to do; no special conditions are needed. You can do it while you are walking to work, on the bus, at the dentist's, or in your own kitchen. Wherever you are, at any moment of the day, you can always glance into yourself and ask yourself: 'How much will it cost to do such or such a thing? Is it really useful?' It is absolutely essential to know exactly what to spend your energies on—I can never over-emphasize this.

Economizing one's energies

Our inner life, just like our outer, physical life, is subject to alternating periods of fruitfulness and sterility, which follow each other, turn and turn about, and if you do not take the proper precautions, you will be like the foolish virgins of the Gospel: when you feel empty and sterile you will cry out in panic: 'I have lost everything I ever had. There is nothing left. All joy and inspiration have deserted me.' Instead of thoughtlessly squandering the wealth you enjoy in your days of plenty, you must remember that there are bound to be difficult days ahead and make provision for them by saving some of your energy for when you need it most.

When you rejoice, therefore, try not to squeeze the very last drop out of your joy. If you do not save some of it, it will soon be followed by tears. Rejoice, but within limits, otherwise you will be like a drunkard staggering home at night: he stumbles against the wall on one side of the street and pushes himself off it only to ricochet off the other side; and so he goes, swaying and staggering from one wall to the other. You must never go to extremes, for one extreme will simply send you back to the other in an eternal see-saw which will rob you of all your energies.

Our relationship with our cells

Initiatic science tells us that each cell of our body is a living creature, a minute, intelligent soul, which breathes and eats, and secretes and projects certain substances. Just think of all the different types of cells in the body and how they all work differently: the cells of the stomach, the brain, the heart, the liver, the sexual organs, and so on, are all specialists in their own particular field. And the sum total of these intelligent little creatures and their activity constitutes our individual intelligence. Yes, our intelligence is built on that of all these tiny cells: we are dependent on them and they on us; together we constitute a unit. On the physical plane we can do nothing without the consent of our cells; the day they stop working, all the different organs and systems of our body—digestion, elimination, respiration, etc.—stop functioning.

Humans beings are the synthesis of the different levels of intelligence that coexist within them. This is why we must get into the habit of 'visiting' our cells and communicating with them. And, you know, they look forward to our visits. They are always there, ready and waiting to serve us, whereas we neglect and abandon them: we do not care one jot for them. People who smoke, for instance, or drink immoderately are damaging the lovely souls that dwell in their heart and lungs; they turn a deaf ear to the complaints and pleas of these cells and continue to ill-treat them, even to the point of making themselves ill.

You must treat your inner population with love and care, and then, if anything starts to go wrong, they will warn you and you can take certain precautions. In this way you will avoid many unpleasant situations. Otherwise no one will warn you of approaching problems, and at the last minute, when it is already too late to take preventive measures, you will wonder why you were not forewarned. But if you know how to relate to your cells, they will keep you informed of the slightest problem, for they love you.

Loving thoughts and kind words can do your organs and limbs a great deal of good. Your health would be greatly improved if you developed the habit of thinking of your cells and talking to them for just a few minutes every day.

Try this exercise: place your hand on your solar plexus and speak to your cells. Ask them to cure all your health problems, but remember to thank them for all the good work they do. You can be sure that they will hear you, because the solar plexus governs all the unconscious functions: secretion, growth, circulation, digestion, elimination, respiration, and so on. In this way you can talk to your cells and they will listen to you, and the greater your faith and your power of thought, the more effective this exercise will be.

Spiritualizing everything we do

Many people imagine that a spiritual person has to devote all his time to prayer and meditation, but this is not so. Whatever work you do, even if it is highly spiritual, becomes extremely prosaic when it is not animated by a very high, sublime ideal, and the reverse is equally true: even the most prosaic, down-to-earth work can become truly spiritual if you know how to inject an element of the divine into it. Spirituality is not a matter of refusing all material, physical activity, but of doing whatever we do for, with, and in the light. Spirituality is a question of knowing how to use all our work in order to rise to greater heights, to become more harmonious, and to attach ourselves more and more firmly to God.

Whatever kind of work you do, even if you can afford only a minute or two at a time, you must get into the habit of renewing your contact with God several times a day. It does not matter if you cannot concentrate for long; it is not the duration that counts but the intensity. Concentrate for just a few seconds and then return to your work; and a little later, you can concentrate again for just a moment or two, and so on.

If you get into the habit of making frequent reference to God and renewing your contact with him, everything you undertake will be more successful. When you begin every activity with a conscious reference to the Lord, the Almighty puts his seal on it. So learn constantly to renew and strengthen your relations with God, wherever you may be, and in this way all your actions will be impregnated with a heavenly influence.

Here is another exercise you can do: every hour on the hour, raise your thoughts to God and say, 'Glory to you, O Lord!' Begin by looking at your watch and repeating this invocation twelve times a day. Later, when it has become a habit with you, you will find it to be an infinitely precious practice: the repetition of these words will give you indescribable joy.

When you are walking, accompany each step you take with the words: wisdom, love; wisdom, love...

When you wash the dishes or sweep a floor, for instance, say, 'Lord, wash my soul as I wash these dishes... Lord, cleanse my heart of all impurities as I clean this floor...'

Whatever you are doing, you can always call on the principles of love, wisdom, and truth so that your activity may be associated with and animated by them. When you are eating, for instance, say, 'The first mouthful is for love, the second is for wisdom, the third is for truth...' When you are getting dressed in the morning, with each garment you put on, say, 'For love... for wisdom... for truth...' And there would be no harm in adding: 'For purity... for justice... for beauty,' and so on.

When your thoughts are occupied by these virtues, you set in motion sublime invisible forces. When you are cooking a meal, every gesture you make is magical, and you can prepare each dish, saying: 'This is for love, this is for wisdom, this is for truth,' and those who eat the meal will be illuminated.

When you touch or move an object, do so as though your whole body were singing and dancing: you will see that the harmony of your gestures will reflect on you throughout the day. People kick the furniture, bang doors, and bump against their chairs, and they do not realize that it is the way they do things that influences their frame of mind. One day, when you are feeling angry or tense, take the opportunity to try this exercise: pick up an object and stroke it gently, caressingly; in no time at all you will find that something inside you has been transformed, that the currents are different.

The importance of harmony

Meditate every day on harmony; love it and long for it so as to introduce it into everything you do: every gesture, every look, every word. In the morning, when you wake up, remember to begin your day by attuning yourself to the world of universal harmony. Your first thought on entering any house should be: 'May peace and harmony reign in this house.'

Let the word 'harmony' soak into you at every moment; keep it within you as a kind of tuning fork: if you feel that you are beginning to worry or get upset, pick it up and listen to it, and do nothing until you have tuned your whole being once more. Harmony is the foundation of every successful venture, every divine realization. Before undertaking any activity, whatever it may be, learn to concentrate on harmony and your work will bear fruit for the rest of eternity.

Learn to say thank you

Human beings are constantly ungrateful not only to God but also to nature and to each other. They do not know that gratitude is a secret force capable of cleansing them and neutralizing the poisons in their bodies.

Try this exercise: all day long, keep repeating the words: 'Thank you, thank you, thank you.' You will object that you will be wasting your time. On the contrary; this is the most useful thing you can ever do with it.

The first thing disciples have to do if they want to reach perfection is to learn to be grateful; this is the key to the transformation of matter—their own matter.

Evening

Each morning is linked to the evening before, and each evening is linked to the morning that follows, and both must be prepared in advance. It is very important not to go to bed in the evening without preparation, for during the night, you will journey into the presence of very elevated, luminous beings in the other world. So you must cleanse and purify yourself and prepare for the voyage.

Evening ablutions

You must wash, of course, before going to bed, but not your face, for you can demagnetize yourself by washing away the beneficial, protective fluids. If you have been doing some very dirty work you can sponge your face with a damp sponge or face-cloth, but do not wash it in running water. Wash your body and your hands and feet, but not your face. In fact, as far as your feet are concerned, it is recommended to wash them in water as hot as you can bear, for a foot-bath has a very beneficial effect on the solar plexus. You do not have to keep your feet in water for long, but wash them consciously, and talk to them as you are washing them. 'Dear feet, I'm afraid I never pay much attention to you, and yet you constantly bear my weight and take me wherever I want to go. I'm just beginning to understand how well you serve me. From now on I shall be more grateful for all your patience and humility.

Preparing for sleep

1. The importance of the last waking moment

Disciples know that the way in which they prepare for sleep is very important, because it is the night that determines what the following day will be. Before going to bed, therefore, they put themselves in touch with the invisible world and lay aside all their worries, cares, and sorrows, all the things that have troubled or pained them during the day. They then call to mind any mistakes they may have made during the day, so as to make up for them during the night, and finally they commend themselves into the hands of the Angel of Death—this is the name that the Cabbalah gives to the Angel of Sleep—for each night we die and each morning we rise from the dead.

To go to sleep, to leave the physical body and journey into the other world, is something we practise every single day in order to be ready when the time comes for our true departure to the other world. Someone who does not know how to go to sleep will not know how to die either. There is no difference between dying and going to sleep, except that when we die we leave our present house for good. In sleep we leave it, but we are still attached to it.

Suppose that during the day you have been happy and well disposed and then, for no apparent reason, just as you are dropping off to sleep, you are besieged by feelings of sadness and discouragement. When you wake up the next morning you will be astonished to see that all the good things you experienced the day before have completely vanished, leaving you with a vague impression of something disagreeable. This shows that it is the experiences of the last minute before you go to sleep that are more important, more significant, than everything that happened during the day. Suppose, on the other hand, that you did not do at all well during the day, but that before going to sleep, you pray and think of something beneficial which helps you to drop off peacefully; those last few minutes of the day will cleanse and purify you so completely that when you wake up next morning you will be full of good intentions and plans for the day.

The innumerable invisible workers that dwell in man make use of the thoughts that are in his mind when he is on the borderline between waking and sleeping, for thoughts set forces in motion. Take care, therefore, never to go to sleep with negative thoughts in your mind, for they will destroy all the good you may have gained during the day. Whereas if you go to sleep with good thoughts in your mind, they will enhance and improve everything within you, and you will be astonished to find yourself in a state of great peace and light when you wake up.

Obviously, this does not mean that you can live as you please during the day as long as you say a prayer before going to sleep; nor that you can wipe out all the evil deeds of a lifetime on your deathbed. No, it is no good thinking you can shake off your devils so easily: they will always be with you. But it is still very important that before going to sleep you manage to pacify and purify yourself and regain inner balance.

If you have dreams in which you do something reprehensible that you would never do when you were awake, it means that you do not know how to prepare yourself for sleep. Before going to sleep you must get ready as though for a sacred pilgrimage which is bound to bear fruit in the near or distant future. The Cabbalah tells us that when someone goes to sleep, an unclean spirit attaches itself to his physical body and tries to suggest certain ideas or desires to him; its purpose is to get hold of his body in order to use the vital forces it harbours. But you can defend yourself from unclean spirits by asking for an angel from heaven to look after you and lead you to the divine school on high, where you will study love and wisdom. In this way, you will always have a guardian to watch over your body at night and prevent evil spirits from taking possession of it.

Anchor a good thought in your mind when you go to bed and leave it to do its work during the night. Never go to bed with a negative thought in your head, for it will wreak havoc in your subconscious.

And what should you do if, before dropping off to sleep, you are suddenly assailed by feelings of anguish or distress? Do not stay in bed; get up, turn on the light and do a few breathing exercises; say a prayer or read something to inspire and encourage you before going back to bed. And if the feeling of distress recurs, get up again and do as before. The thing to realize is that you cannot win the battle when you are lying down. You may be afraid of catching cold if you get up and may

Think that you can perfectly well win a mental battle while remaining snug and warm in bed. No, you have to be extremely strong to defend yourself when lying down. In a horizontal position one is much weaker and more passive; when one is upright one is stronger and can act with greater freedom.

2. Exercises and prayers at bedtime

The Master Peter Deunov recommended the following formula to be said at night, before going to bed. Place your open right hand, palm down, on your solar plexus, and the back of your open left hand on your back, on the same level, and say, three times:

> God is light within me,
> My spirit is warmth,
> I am kindness.

> God is light within me,
> The angels are warmth,
> Human beings are kindness.

And here is the same formula in Bulgarian for anyone who is interested:

> *Gospod văv mene é svetlina*
> *Anguelité să toplina*
> *Čelovecité să dobrina.*

> *Gospod văv mene é svetlina*
> *Douhăt mi é toplina*
> *Az săm dobrina.*

You can also pronounce the following formula:
'My God, let me enrol tonight in your school of love,

wisdom, and truth and learn to serve you better, so that your kingdom and your righteousness may be established on earth.'

Meditate for a few moments and then, with your right hand, trace the outline of a pentagram in the air, as shown below.

3. Direction and position

The position you adopt when sleeping is also very important. In the first place, it is preferable to sleep with your head towards the North or the East. Do not sleep face down nor flat on your back, because this causes the body wastes to settle in the spine; nor on the left side because of the heart. The best position is on your right side, because in this way the wastes drain towards the liver, which can then do its work of eliminating them. It does not matter if you change your position in the night, but it is best to start the night lying on your right side.

4. Sleeplessness

Instead of closing your eyes and struggling for hours to get to sleep, make up your mind that you want to stay awake. Get up and work until you feel more peaceful.

Alternatively, you can stay in bed, but with your eyes wide open. Look into the dark with the firm intention of remaining wide awake all night, and you will soon find that you are beginning to drop off. When you notice this, renew your effort to keep your eyes wide open. In this way sleep will not be long in coming to you, whereas if you try to drop off by keeping your eyes closed you will not succeed.

There are other methods you can use as well: one of them is to drink some hot water, and another is to massage your solar plexus with a circular motion, anti-clockwise.

5. The meaning of sleep for a disciple

When they go to sleep, true disciples leave their physical bodies behind and go to join their master and continue to learn from him. They read the most secret books in the libraries of the universe and attend great and splendid ceremonies. Sometimes, although the human brain is not built to retain the memory of such things, disciples have some recollection of these ceremonies in the morning. They leave such an impression of sweetness and peace in the heart that, upon waking, the disciple exclaims, 'I don't know where I was last night, but it was so beautiful. Really heavenly!' Sleep becomes something sacred when one goes to bed with the intention of going to the other world to study reality, for it is there that one receives true initiation.

Chapter Three

Nutrition

Every day, in the morning, at noon, and again in the evening, we all have to think about eating in order to sustain life and health. But initiates are the only ones who have paused to reflect on this phenomenon. Their age-old science has taught them that nutrition is extremely important and that there are many aspects to the question, aspects that most human beings are totally unaware of. And it is this ignorance that is the source of many of their problems.

The importance of one's attitude

Always remember to wash your hands before eating. Then try to put yourself into a calm, peaceful frame of mind and remind yourself that you are about to receive elements that have been prepared for you in the immense laboratories of nature. Recollect yourself for a moment, renew your contact with the Lord and say a short prayer,[1] and then, silently and in all serenity, begin the process of nutrition, a process which constitutes one of the highest forms of white magic.

1.See page 30.

Mastication

You must chew your food for as long possible until there is nothing left in your mouth, even without having swallowed. The mouth is the first 'laboratory' in which the food you eat is processed, and it is also the most important and the most spiritual. The stomach is of secondary importance. The subtlest processes are carried out in the mouth, for it is in the laboratory of the mouth that the etheric particles are absorbed, whereas the coarser, denser elements are sent on to the stomach. In fact, one often feels strengthened long before a meal has been absorbed and digested and the nutrients distributed to the various organs of the body, and this proves that even before the food has reached the stomach, the mouth has extracted the etheric elements from it and distributed them to the nervous system.

Nourishing our subtle bodies

Nourishment consists, first of all, in consciously extracting the elements needed to build up our physical bodies from the food we eat. But human beings are not restricted to only one, physical body: they have other, subtler bodies which, owing to human ignorance, are frequently under-nourished. So the important question is how to nourish these subtle bodies. Everybody knows more or less what their physical body needs, but they have no idea how to nourish their etheric or vital body, their astral body (seat of the emotions and feelings), or their mental body (seat of thought).[2]

1. The etheric body

As I have said, we have to masticate our food very thoroughly. But mastication is for the benefit of the physical body. If we want to nourish our etheric body, we must add another factor, that of respiration. From time to time in the course of your meal, you must pause and take a deep breath; this

---

2.See *Complete Works*, vol. 2, for fuller explanations concerning the subtle bodies.

is the only way to ensure that the etheric body gets the subtler particles it needs from your food. But if you are so busy talking and arguing that you swallow your food automatically without taking the time to chew it, you will disturb the rhythm of your breathing and the necessary physico-chemical reactions will not occur as they should, with the result that you will have a feeling of heaviness and discomfort: proof positive that you are not eating correctly. In order to nourish your etheric body, therefore, you must also eat in silence.

2. *The astral body*

The astral body is nourished by thoughts and emotions, a form of matter that is even subtler than the particles of the etheric plane. We nourish our astral body by the love and respect we feel for the food prepared for us in the Lord's laboratories. When our astral body is nourished by these elements it is capable of arousing in us feelings of a very high order: love for all human beings and a sensation of being happy and at peace and in harmony with nature.

If you give your astral body the food it needs, you will have a tremendous sense of well-being and generosity, and when you have important questions to settle with others, you will be ready to make concessions and act with magnanimity, patience, and benevolence. On the other hand, when you spend your mealtime grumbling and being angry and critical of others, your astral body does not get the nourishment it needs, and you continue to feel tense, bad-tempered, and biased, and if you have a difficult problem to resolve, you will make a negative, unjust decision. Later you will have to apologize and excuse yourself: 'I can't help it. My nerves are in a terrible state!' It will not do you any good to swallow quantities of pills in the hope of calming your nerves; you will go on being tense and irritable until you have learned the importance of the way you eat for your physical and psychic health.

3. The mental body

Disciples nourish the mental body by concentrating mentally on the food they are eating. Instead of looking round and watching other people, they close their eyes to avoid being distracted and to be free to devote complete attention to their food. To disciples, food is a manifestation of God, a love letter from the Lord, and for this reason they try to read the messages hidden in it, and to dwell on all its different aspects: where it comes from, what it contains, the qualities that correspond to it, the entities that have cultivated and cared for it, and so on. Disciples know that there are entities that care for every single plant and every fruit, and that if they mature and ripen at a particular moment, it means that there is a correspondence with specific planetary influences. Disciples' minds are occupied in profound meditation of all these things while they are eating, and in this way, their mental bodies are nourished by elements that are even subtler and of a higher order than those of the astral plane. The result is that they gain greatly in lucidity and clarity of thought and acquire a more profound grasp of life and of the world. After a meal taken in these conditions, disciples leave the table with luminous understanding and the capability of undertaking extremely arduous intellectual tasks.

4. The causal, buddhic and atmic bodies

Above and beyond their etheric, astral, and mental bodies, human beings have other, subtler bodies, the causal, buddhic, and atmic bodies, and they, too, have to be nourished. Perhaps you wonder how. In addition to breathing deeply and eating their food with love and meditating on it, initiates cultivate a profound sense of gratitude to the Creator; through their food, they achieve communion with the Lord. In this way they nourish their three higher bodies and experience rapture and ecstasies.

Never eat your fill

You all know that it is very bad to overeat: there is nothing worse than being sated and gorged after a meal, for it makes you heavy and coarse. But what you do not know is that hunger prolongs, strengthens, and enhances life. If you still have some appetite left when you leave the table, it is an incentive to your etheric body to look for other, subtler elements in the surrounding atmosphere. Think of these elements as etheric hormones, or vitamins if you like, which your etheric body finds and absorbs, and quite soon after, not only do you no longer feel hungry but you feel lighter, more vigorous, and better able to tackle your work. Whereas if you eat more than your hunger warrants, simply for the pleasure of eating (as so many people do at a banquet or a party, for instance), you will feel weighed down and incapable of working.

When you eat your fill you overburden yourself; your etheric body gets tired and overworked and ceases to function properly. Then myriads of importunate, undesirable entities of the astral plane, who have been attracted by the glut of food, come flocking into you to claim their share. This is why, very soon after, you feel hungry all over again; so you eat again, and once again those undesirable guests return. In this way you become a tempting morsel for the famished entities of the lower astral regions who come and feast on you.

The whole universe abounds in creatures of every sort and kind which initiates have grouped into specific categories, and they often intervene in the lives of human beings. This explains many unusual events and phenomena which continue to puzzle today's scientists. If you do not want to fall a prey to these undesirable creatures, therefore, you must be careful not to eat your fill, not to overstep the limit.

Food bestows the gift of eternal life

Why we bless our food

Observe your attitude and reactions while you are eating and they will give you an accurate idea of your degree of evolution. If you have no respect for the food that God has given you, how can you expect to have respect for anything else? When you have learned to respect your food you will begin to understand what Jesus meant when he said, 'Take, eat; this is my body; drink, this is my blood,' and, 'He who eats my flesh and drinks my blood has eternal life.'[3] That the food we eat has already been blessed and consecrated by the Lord himself is evident from the fact that it is capable of giving us life. God is in food in the form of life. You must not think that food needs to be blessed by human beings before it can give us life; no, long before man blessed food it was already blessed by heaven. God is life, and if food gives us life, it is because it contains God.

Perhaps you will say, 'Does this mean that we should not say grace and bless the food before a meal?' No, not at all; you are right to bless your food. But first of all you must know what a blessing is and what effect it has. A blessing is a ceremony, a magic rite. Through the words, gestures and thoughts of the person who gives the blessing, the food is enclosed and immersed in fluidic emanations which prepare it for consumption by bringing it into harmony with those who are going to eat it. In this way there is contact and adaptation on the level of the subtle bodies, and the beneficial elements contained in the food become more readily available. However, the powers of a human blessing are limited. If it were so easy to impregnate matter with divine life, you could bless wood or metal or a stone, and then eat it! True, you can bless objects made of wood, stone, or metal, and in doing so, you can inject an element of life into them, but it will not be a degree of life sufficient to nourish

3.See *Complete Works*, vol. 1, chap. 5.

human beings. It may have other effects on them, but it cannot nourish them.

If food gives us life it is because it already contains the life that the Creator gave it, but that life needs to be raised to a higher degree and stimulated and enhanced by our blessings, above all by our gratitude. We eat in order to obtain the life that God—or, if you prefer, nature—has placed in food. A meal is like the conception of a child. In giving us food, Christ gives us life, and by our consciousness of what we are doing, of the fact that we are consuming the body and blood of Christ, we enter into communion with his spirit.

It is more than likely that you have never before envisaged the nutritional process in this way. But henceforth, with the coming of the new race of humanity, I can tell you that human beings will be instructed in these methods; they will learn that nutrition is not the humble, commonplace, contemptible process they thought, but that within this everyday act of eating, God has concealed the possibility of doing psychic work of the utmost importance. They will understand that nutrition can be a means to perfection.

Chapter Four

Actions

Le Bonfin

The magical power of a gesture

Human beings are made up of several different bodies which are of subtler material than the physical body, and these subtle bodies are the medium through which we make contact with a great many forces, intelligent spirits, and entities in the universe. These forces and intelligences often express themselves through a person's gestures, movements, and facial expressions, and, conversely, whether they know that they are doing so or not, people put themselves in touch with these entities when they make certain gestures or assume certain postures.

Magic is the science of gestures. For this reason, disciples must learn to be conscious of every movement they make; they must be careful not to make useless or destructive gestures while they are talking or walking or in their work, for they can have very grave consequences from the spiritual point of view. Every gesture is a force, and it is operative on every level of being; it corresponds to specific currents, colours, and vibrations and affects a host of beings in and around us. Every gesture opens or closes certain doors of nature to us and links us either to good or evil powers. If we want to advance on the path of love, wisdom, and truth, we must study our gestures and see whether they manifest the presence of these three virtues within us.

The way you walk

It is very important to be aware of how you walk. You must walk with a light, elastic step, keeping your head up. It is a bad sign to walk bent, with your eyes on the ground, or to pound the ground heel first at every step. People who walk like that do not realize what violence they are inflicting on their brains, but it will not be long before they damage their nervous systems, and this will influence the way they think and everything they do, which will show signs of violence and coarseness.

When you set out for a long walk you should not carry anything in your hands. You can carry whatever you need on your back, but leave your hands free. Refrain from talking or singing; adjust your steps to the rhythm of your breathing and allow your arms to swing freely as you walk, as though they were helping you to advance. This movement of the arms combined with your rhythmic breathing will enable you to walk for a long time without tiring.

Of course it is also important to have an idea in your head. If you are walking through a forest, for instance, you might say, 'May all those who pass through this forest be moved by love and the spirit of brotherhood. May it be beneficial to them. May they grow to be children of God and work for peace.' Or if you are on an excursion in the mountains, think of the light that you will find up at the top, of how you will be nearer to heaven, and you will return home purified and transformed.

The hands

A great many people have the habit of gesticulating with their hands while they are talking. It is sometimes extremely trying, when you are talking to someone, to see the ceaseless, incoherent movements of their hands, or to watch them nervously fiddling with an object, twisting a lock of hair or plucking at a button on their clothes. It is impossible to concentrate on what they are saying, and, after only a few minutes one feels utterly exhausted.

You must educate your hands and learn how to use them in ways that will help yourself and others. There are all kinds of exercises you can do for this purpose.

1. Exercises with the hands

1. With the palm of your right hand, stroke the back of your left hand very, very gently, barely touching it.

2. With the tips of the first three fingers of your right hand, stroke each finger of your left hand, beginning with the thumb.

3. Hold your right hand open in front of you, concentrate on the centre of the palm for a moment and then, very slowly, close your fingers to form a fist, all the while concentrating on the movement of the fingers. Keep your fist closed for a moment while you concentrate all your strength in it and then, very gradually, open your fingers again. Do this exercise with great attention, once a day. Once is enough; you will not become any stronger by doing it twenty times in a row. But do it properly every day.

It is not necessary to perform difficult or spectacular exercises. Get it into your heads, once and for all, that the secret of true power lies in little things.

Our fingers are antennae; each one receives and transmits currents or waves of a particular nature. Initiates know how to use their fingers to tune in to the currents that flow through space, and, in this way, they are able to purify and heal not only themselves but other people as well.

But the hands pick up all kinds of impurities very easily, so it is important to wash them frequently if they are to function properly as antennae. However, the physical water with which you wash your physical hands cannot really do this adequately:

you have to use spiritual water. As often as you can think of it, imagine a stream of spiritual water, a torrent of light and pure colour, pouring over your hands, and hold them under it for as long as possible.

2. Shaking hands

A handshake, also, is a gesture of considerable importance in our daily encounters with others. We should shake hands only once, not two or three times in rapid succession. Why? Because when we shake hands for the first time there is a mutual exchange of gifts, but if we shake hands a second time we take back what we have given. With the first handshake we give each other something very subtle; with the second handshake we exchange denser, more material currents, and with the third and fourth handshakes we give each other the dregs. With the first draught we drink what is most spiritual, but with each succeeding draught we get closer to the sediment, the slime that has settled on the bottom. You may object that it all depends; each case is different. Yes, that is true, but that does not make the general rule any less valid.

When you shake hands with someone you should do so consciously and very lovingly. If you are thinking of something else, you would do better not to shake hands at all.

3. The salute[1]

A magus is a being who knows how to use his hands not only to tune in to the forces that surround him in space but also to project, channel, and orientate them, or to amplify or reduce their power. We are in the habit of raising our hand to salute each other several times a day. This is a deeply significant and efficacious gesture, but only if you are fully conscious of what

1.In the salute exchanged between the Master and the members of the Brotherhood, the right arm is raised in an easy, supple gesture, the open hand level with or slightly higher than one's head, the palm turned towards the person one is greeting.

you are doing, and if your eyes and your hand are brimming over with love that you project for the benefit of the whole world. Our salute should be potent, harmonious, and alive—a true communion.

The eyes

Theoretically, the eyes are purely passive, receptive organs. However, it is possible to use your eyes to give, not only to receive. Yes, the eyes can be emissive, they can talk, suggest, influence, command, and even kill.

1. How to look at others

One should never importune others by staring at them fixedly. On the other hand, one should not look at others with lifeless, expressionless eyes. If there is too much passivity in the way you look at others, they will feel not only that they are not receiving anything from you but that they are being drained of their energies.

You must observe the way you look at others and be careful of the expression in your eyes, asking yourself whether you are giving or taking. It is good to give and it is also good to take in exchange. But if you only take, if you suck other people dry like a vampire, you will always be unwelcome wherever you go, because you will be a spiritual thief. Whereas those who train themselves to radiate light and give comfort to others by their look practise the highest form of magic. The only thing that has the power to open the gates of heaven to us is our desire to give, to make others happy—the intense desire to serve the divine cause.

You should look at others gently but without insistence, so as to leave them free. Do not try to force them to respond to your look or to manifest themselves according to your wishes, for if you thrust your will on others they will feel it as an aggression, a violation. In any case, you cannot force people to open their hearts to you; they will always resist if you try to use coercion. The secret to winning the hearts and souls of others is love, a disinterested love that shuns the use of violence.

Study this question as it manifests itself in your own family and social life, and you will see that a great many things depend on the way in which people look at each other. The influence that a look can have on a person's destiny has never been sufficiently studied. You must not think that it is such a tiny detail that it cannot be significant. A look is a synthesis of the entire person; it contains and reflects them in their entirety: the refinement or coarseness of their nature, their stupidity or intelligence, the nobility or baseness of their character, their strength and their weakness. A person's look is an epitome of their whole being and it leaves its imprint wherever it rests. If you want to change your manner of looking at others you will have to change your whole existence, the way in which you think, feel, and act. A look is a channel through which energies are poured out on living and inanimate creatures alike. Innumerable destinies have been changed and devastated by a single look.

2. Some recommendations

When you are angry with someone, there is always the tendency to give them a furious look. Be careful! You must never look at someone with hostility; if you find yourself in this situation, rather than devastating someone with a look, close your eyes and try to transform the force of anger within you. If you look at someone with anger or hostility, without knowing it you are projecting a force that will one day be turned against you.

Try not to look down for too long either, for when you look at the ground you are putting yourself in contact with the powers of earth. Of course, I am not saying that you should walk about gazing at the sky—that would be exaggerated. But realize that when you have been looking at someone while talking to them, it is very bad suddenly to look down at the ground.

If you want to see what someone is doing, turn your face towards them; do not look at them sideways. It is a very bad habit to look at people out of the corner of your eyes: it reveals a lack of sincerity and openness.

One must never hide one's eyes during a conversation with someone else. The Master Peter Deunov reprimanded one of his disciples very severely one day for putting his hand in front of his eyes while he was talking to him. You must never do that, for it raises a barrier between the outer world and the inner gaze.

3. How to help others with a look

It is important to know that you can help people simply by looking at them. If someone is in doubt, distress, or despair, you can help them with a look. Everywhere, wherever you go, in buses or trains or in the street, you are always meeting people that you can help by looking at them with kindness while you send them a thought to encourage them and put some heart into them. At the time they will not realize what you have done for them, but their souls and the spiritual entities within them will know how to welcome what you send them, and they will feel the better for it.

Words

You must be extremely careful about the words that pass your lips, because even if you really mean no harm, evil entities can use the matter supplied by something negative you say in order to make it a reality. You cannot blame them for that; it is up to you not to supply them with the means to do evil.

There are many countries in which people are in the habit of cursing others: on the slightest pretext they will call down curses on their parents, their children, or their neighbours. It is a very bad habit, because these words create the right conditions for disaster. So be very watchful in this respect; also, never end a conversation on a negative note, for there is a law which ensures that the last words you utter continue to have negative repercussions. Even if you are obliged to say something critical about someone, do not end by dwelling on their faults; otherwise, by virtue of the same law, the evil effects of your words will devastate you even before they touch them. End on a positive note, saying, 'But still, they do have some good points.' Mention them, and then stop talking.

What exactly is a word? A word is a rocket launched into space that sets certain forces in motion, arousing certain entities and producing irreversible effects along its path. Yes, the effects produced by a word are irreparable. Obviously, if it were possible to remedy the effects of an ill-chosen word at once it would not do any harm, but the destructive effects increase as time passes. Time, therefore, is an extraordinarily important factor. Suppose you have given orders for somebody's head to be chopped off and those who have been commissioned to do the deed are already on their way: what can you possibly do to repair things once your enemy's head has rolled in the dust? Can you glue it on again? What can you do about an order once it has been given? The only thing to do is to countermand it, to send other messengers to stop the executioners before it is too late. But if you wait too long there will be nothing you can do to repair the damage. This is why the Bible warns us not to let the sun go down on our anger; it means that when we have wronged someone we must make reparation as soon as possible. Most human beings let their feelings boil over and say whatever comes into their heads, but one day karma is going to knock on their door and call them to account. So you must make reparation immediately: do not wait even one day, because a word has wings; it is an active force, a power that reaches out into space.

However, you must know that there is a force that is more rapid and more efficacious even than a word, and that is thought. If you set your thoughts to work immediately, they can overtake your words. It is not easy, of course, because thought belongs to a far subtler region than words, but if you sincerely want to counteract the harmful effects of your words, you can do so by concentrating deeply and asking some servants of the invisible world to prevent them from causing any harm. You cannot completely repair the damage you have done, but you can prevent the worst from happening. You can avoid the worst, that is, if you act very quickly and if your thought is strong and very intense. Otherwise the warrant for the execution will have been carried out before you can get it back, your victim will have lost his head (symbolically speaking), and one day you will have to pay for the evil you have done.

A prayer:

Lord God, forgive me for not having understood sooner the powers and possibilities you have placed in my mouth; for not having understood that every time I speak I have the power to imitate you, to become like you, to be a reflection of you. I never realized it before and have used the gift of speech to do harm: I have talked nonsense; I have hurt people; I have used this instrument to upset other creatures and create havoc. Instead of using it to do good, to console, relieve, guide, vivify, and resuscitate others and to stimulate and lead them to you, our Lord and Creator, I have used it to destroy and defile them. Forgive me, Lord, and teach me to use my tongue and my mouth not merely to eat and chatter mindlessly, but to do good and to warm and enlighten others.

Thoughts and feelings

Human beings are ceaselessly engaged in creating thoughts and feelings, both good and bad. They do not realize that these thoughts and feelings are tiny living creatures, and that once they have brought them into the world they are going to have to nourish them. Yes, these creatures survive by feeding on the very substance of their creator. If they are bad they drain him of all his energies, and if they are good they bring him all kinds of gifts.

If you have a pack of rowdy, violent, undisciplined children who spend their time creating havoc in the neighbourhood, passers-by, your next-door neighbours, and even the police will come and complain and demand that you exercise better control over them. Parents are responsible for their children and their mischief; it is they who have to repair and pay compensation for any damage they may do. Well, our inner world is full of our own rowdy 'children', creatures that we have given birth to, and who constantly do all kinds of damage because they have been engendered by our own obscure, evil motives and intentions. One day cosmic law will come and demand that we pay for the damage they have done.

But nobody except the great masters ever tells human beings these truths, and they are forever tormented by the same question: 'Why am I always harassed and tormented and unhappy?' The answer is simple: it is your own children who torment you. It was your own hatred, anger, and desire for revenge that gave birth to them. Like God himself, you are really and truly a creator—not only in the physical dimension but on every level.

True morality is based on the realization that we are responsible for everything we do—not only physically but also on the astral and mental planes. True morality is not a question of conforming outwardly to a certain set of rules; it is a question of getting into the habit of constantly creating a multitude of useful, beneficial, luminous thoughts and feelings, and of sending them out, day and night, to do good to every being in the universe. These little creatures sent out by our hearts and souls may be invisible, but that does not prevent them from being very real and capable of doing a great deal of good.

Correct your mistakes

Every thought, feeling, and action, whether good or bad, is recorded within us. Of course, it is impossible not to make some negative or defective recordings, but at least you can try to be aware of what you are doing and to take steps to make amends.

Nobody is immune from the danger of saying or thinking something bad about somebody, but the important thing is to realize at once what you have done and to repair the damage.

Chapter Five

Overcoming the Evil Within

Weaknesses and vices

Danger signals

Let us suppose that you have a failing, a weakness that continually gets the better of you. Perhaps you are too fond of alcohol or women; perhaps you are inclined to speak ill of others, to squander your money on rubbish, or to amuse yourself when you should be working, and so on. Whatever it may be, there are always certain signs which precede the onslaught of temptation, and you must learn to recognize them and be warned by them. You can do this by looking back to the times when this failing manifested itself in the past, and by identifying the signs and circumstances that preceded these incidents. You may find that the warning takes the form of a tenseness in your solar plexus, a feeling of discomfort, or a thought or image that springs spontaneously into your mind.

Everybody is warned by certain signs, but they differ from one person to the next, so you have to look for and identify your own. Once you have put your finger on your own particular danger signals, you are in a position to get the upper hand of your weakness, for as soon as they appear you will know that you have to be on your guard and take the necessary precautions. But to do this you have to be free; if you are the slave of too many absorbing, fascinating activities, they will deaden your perceptions and prevent you from seeing into yourself.

Your attitude towards your own vices

It is not good .constantly to remember the faults one has committed, unless it be in order to learn from them so as to do better in the future. Forget all the old things of the past; stop talking about them; stop trying to show your humility by beating your breast before the Lord and telling him that you are a sinner. The Lord has no need to hear all that. On the contrary, you should say, 'Lord, I am your child, help me to acquire your wisdom, strength, and light; help me to overcome my difficulties so that I may glorify you on earth as the angels glorify you in heaven.' True humility does not consist in continually condemning oneself for one's sins, but in refusing to take the credit for even one's most glorious deeds, and in saying, 'The glory for this deed belongs not to me, O Lord, but to your holy name.'

Learn to use the forces of evil[1]

It is because human beings have never understood evil that they are always trying to destroy it. But we must not destroy evil; we must absorb it and make use of it in our work. Chemists do not try to destroy poisonous substances: they use them. And nature never rejects or destroys anything: she takes refuse and wastes and uses them as raw materials with which to produce flowers and fruit.

Human beings, who have still not understood this important truth, are always begging God to destroy evil, but God just smiles and scratches his head and murmurs, 'Poor creatures!

1.For a fuller discussion of good and evil see *Complete Works*, vol. 5, chaps. 3 and 4.

When they begin to understand that evil is necessary, they will stop begging me to do away with it!' But how many prayers are still going to be said before that day comes? True, we should pray, but we should pray to understand God's point of view: 'Lord God, help me to understand your conception of the world and the plan you had in mind when you created it, so that, like you, I may be above evil and unscathed by it; so that I may learn to use it to accomplish something really glorious.' If you can start to think along these lines, you will soon discover that nothing in nature is bad. Instead of struggling to rid themselves once and for all of the negative forces that torment them, disciples must learn to use them to become stronger and stronger.

Religious and moral doctrines are in error when they say that we have to tear out evil by the roots, for evil contains tremendous powers, without which man can only become weaker.

Let me give you some examples:

1. Sexual energy

It will help you to understand sexual energy if you compare it to petrol. Those who are ignorant or who handle it carelessly get burned: it is a force that consumes their quintessence. Whereas those who know how to handle it can use it to fly into space. There is no better illustration of this question of sexual energy. And why not learn to fly to the stars and explore the whole of creation instead of continually getting burned?

There is a new philosophy in the world today. It is a philosophy that teaches men and women how to regard each other, how to use the excitement and delight they inspire in each other to become exceptional beings, capable of the most exalted achievements, because they are nourished, sustained, and propelled to celestial heights by love.

2. Vanity

There is nothing basically wrong with the desire to show oneself in the best possible light. In fact you could say that it is nature herself who has planted this tendency in the heart of human beings in order to oblige them to evolve. Sometimes, in their desire to win the approval and admiration of others, people are led to surpass themselves; many have conquered fear and won acclaim as heroes simply because they could not bear to let their family or their country down. Artists are constantly spurred on to greater heights of perfection in their art by the thought that otherwise their public might tire of them and their work. In any case, all parents, teachers, and educators make use of this tendency in children in order to stimulate them to work better. When you show children that you trust them to work well, that you expect great things of them, they will do their best to live up to your expectations. You can even help delinquents to work well if you give them responsibility and make them feel that you really trust them. Vanity, therefore, is an excellent tendency as long as it is used to further one's evolution.

3. Doubt

You seem to feel the need to doubt absolutely everything! Well, instead of always doubting the existence of God, the wisdom of cosmic intelligence, or the generosity of others, why not try to be a little less sure of yourself and doubt your own infallibility? Why not ask yourself from time to time: 'Am I always right? Do I always know exactly what is true or untrue? Is there not another way of reasoning which might be better than mine?' How will you ever know if you do not start looking for it? Unfortunately, when it comes to one's own opinion, there is no room for doubt.

Human beings doubt everything except their own powers of reasoning, and this is why they are always getting into trouble. Is this an intelligent way to behave? Instead of being so sure that all their desires and ambitions are perfectly valid and, indeed, highly commendable, and being ready to spring to their defence, they should start asking themselves whether they are really as legitimate and divine as they like to believe. Instead of always doubting their higher nature, their own spirit and the gifts that God has given them, let them doubt their own lower nature. Unfortunately, they doubt the means of salvation that God has given them, and have absolute trust in the forces that run wild within them. Since human beings are so bent on doubting, they should at least know what to doubt.

Spiritual grafting[2]

Suppose you have a wild pear tree which produces only hard, inedible fruit: you can graft a slip from a cultivated pear tree on to it and it will give you a crop of magnificent fruit. Human beings have become past-masters in techniques of this kind, but when it comes to the psychic or spiritual domain, they are not nearly so capable or ingenious.

1. Sensuality

Suppose, for instance, that you have a very loving but very sensual nature. Your love is a formidable, irresistible force, but it is wild and untamed; you need to graft a cutting from a pure, noble, disinterested love on to it. In this way, the energies of your lower nature will rise and circulate through the new branches—that is, through the new circuits etched into your brain—and produce magnificent fruit, the fruit of a prodigious love which will enrapture and inspire you in ways you never thought possible.

2.See also chap. 9.

2. Vanity

If your vanity is really excessive and absorbs a lot of your time and energy, there, too, you can give it a new direction. Instead of always trying to be great and glorious in the eyes of the world, in the eyes of gossips and idle onlookers, you can still seek glory, but a divine glory that will never fade or tarnish because you put it in the service of a heavenly goal.

3. Anger

If you are very hot-tempered, it is more than likely that, in a fit of rage, you have already destroyed more than one friendship and spoiled your chances of promotion. Well, instead of letting blind anger burst from you like a thunderbolt, you can transform and sublimate it with a graft and become tireless in the battle against all that is inferior—a true soldier of Christ, a valiant servant of God. Instead of using your Martian energies to destroy all that is good, you can use them to do something constructive.

All you have to do is find some cuttings. But do not forget that you must be sure to keep the roots and stem of your wild plant; you must never attempt to tear them out, for they are vigorous and full of life, and your new cuttings are going to be grafted on to them. Mentally, you are going to draw on these lower energies and link them to a higher entity, a spirit of light, an angel, or an archangel.

All the initiates have had to perform grafts by allying themselves with beings of a higher order, and the fruits they bore as a result were sweeter and more fragrant. But the most powerful and most sublime graft of all is to unite yourself to the Lord, saying: 'Dear Lord, I want to work for the coming of your kingdom and your righteousness, but I can do so little on my own. I beg you to come and dwell in me and to work and manifest yourself through me.' This is the best, the most sublime graft possible, and if God grants your prayer and binds you to himself, your tree—by which I mean you, yourself—which produced nothing but bitter, inedible fruit in the past, will start producing sweet, juicy, fragrant fruit. All that remains of the original 'tree' are the roots and the trunk, but the cutting grafted on to it, that is, the divine, invisible world, heaven itself, produces fruits of its own. How does this happen? When all those raw, turbulent energies are pledged to the service of the Lord by means of a spiritual graft, he takes them for his own and transforms them.

Sexuality

Let me give you just two examples of spiritual grafting in the domain of sexuality.

One day I had a visit from a young girl. She was very pretty and attractive and, judging from her manners, very well brought up, but she was utterly miserable because she was obsessed by the image of the male sexual organs: whatever she set her eyes on—flowers, fruit, household objects, even the ceiling—the only thing she saw was this. The phenomenon was all the more painful to her because she was a Catholic, so she felt terribly guilty and sinful and thought that God must certainly reject her. When she explained all this I began to laugh, and she looked at me in astonishment. So then I said, 'You must not let this upset you; there is nothing grave or sinful in what you have told me. It is all quite natural and normal; it is the kind of thing that happens to some extent to everybody. There is no cause for despair. It is nature's business to see that the human species does not disappear, so she creates these images in the minds of men and women. However, you have to learn what use to make of them; otherwise, just look at what a state you can get into.'

'Now, what should you do the next time this image comes into your mind? Instead of getting all upset, look at it calmly. Do not dwell on it for too long, for then you might start to feel certain desires which could lead to your doing something to console yourself. To avoid that danger, you have to indulge in a little philosophy—that is, you have to start thinking of the sublime cosmic intelligence that inspired the formation of these organs. As you reflect and meditate on this, you will be moved to admiration for this sublime intelligence that has created such perfection, and you will forget all about any temptations that these images might have given you. Whereas, if you continue to dwell on them and worry about them, you will never free yourself. Use the image that comes into your mind as a springboard that can catapult you all the way to the Godhead. If you did not have an occasional springboard like that, how would you ever reach your predestined goal on high? Occasions like this are magnificent opportunities, for they give you a new lift, a new impetus. But do not forget that you must use them simply as a jumping-off place; otherwise you will get hopelessly entangled and lose your bearings entirely.'

Unfortunately, human beings do not know how to take that extra step that would enable them to reflect and see the wonder of these things; they fail to realize that it is this wonder and admiration that can be their salvation. They say, 'What on earth is wrong with me? It's horrible. Disgusting!' and this is where they get lost. Get rid of the notion that it is 'disgusting' and begin to see the beauty and wonder of what nature has formed with such supreme intelligence. It is this state of wonder that will enable you to solve your problem.

My second example is this: A few days ago I had a visit from a man of a certain age who confessed to a terrible weakness: whenever he found himself in the presence of a woman he simply could not restrain himself, and he wanted to know what he could do to remedy the problem. My answer was this: 'In the first place, you should have begun to think about that a long time ago. However, I can give you some exercises that you can try. Go to the beach, for instance, and look at all the pretty girls sunbathing; obviously, when you do that, it will arouse something in you. That is normal; you cannot expect anything else. But as you cannot do anything to satisfy your desire—you do not know any of them and there are too many people about, anyway—you will be forced to resist temptation and make the effort to sublimate it. In this way you can begin to exercise your will, and if you do this exercise successfully several times, you will not even have to go to the beach any more. You can do it at home by looking at certain magazines: here, too, something will be aroused in you, and you can grasp the sensation as you feel it coming on and send it upwards, all the way to the divine Mother. If you practise like this for a long time, you will no longer need physical relations with women, and you will have gained the victory and triumphed over your weakness. But you have to practise using homoeopathic doses in this way for a long time. A homoeopathic remedy can be 'potentized' to the ninth centesimal and still be extremely effective. Love, too, can be potentized to such a degree that one no longer needs the physical contact, and at that point it becomes spiritual love. As you can see, it is simply a question of knowing how to set about it: instead of running away from the problem and remaining vulnerable, you must take the bull by the horns.'[3]

Forming new habits

Your faults and failings are patterns which are deeply ingrained within you, and whatever you do, they are always with you, urging you to repeat the same actions over and over again. You can struggle against them all your life, but you can never completely vanquish them. The only way to free yourself from your old habits is to develop new ones, by adopting a new attitude and cultivating new thoughts and feelings. In this way you will be establishing new patterns. But there is one thing you have to understand, and that is that when you develop new patterns, it does not mean that the old ones have disappeared.

3.See *Complete Works*, vol. 14, chap. 2.

No, they never disappear; they are only buried under layers of new ones. As long as you continue to behave in accordance with your new orientation, the old patterns will remain in the background, but if you slide back and relax your vigilance, they will come up to the surface again.

Take the case of a man who decides he is going to stop seducing women: if he has not acquired a new inner attitude, at the first opportunity he will slide back into his old habit. Full of remorse and disappointed with himself, he will be utterly miserable and swear that next time things will be different. But when the next time comes it will be exactly like the last. If he really wants it to be different, he is going to have to change something in his looks and words and gestures, and if he can succeed just once, he has a good chance of succeeding a second and a third time, for every time he succeeds, the new pattern is etched more deeply. We can use this method to rid ourselves of all the negative tendencies that plague us: anger, slanderous gossip, greed, laziness, and so on.

Negative moods

Stop and redirect your thoughts

Suppose that you are at work one day and you wonder why things are not going as they should. If you think about it, you realize that when you began you were in a state of nervous tension. In this case, you must stop whatever you are doing. If you fail to stop, your nervous tension will continue indefinitely. So interrupt your work for a moment, and then begin again to a new rhythm, and this new state will endure in place of the first.

Why do people slam doors, kick the furniture, and bang things about when they are angry? Because they are unable to control the force within them, so they try to get rid of it by physical violence. The only trouble is that the more they give way to their fury, the worse it gets. The solution is to do just the opposite: to keep perfectly still for a moment or two, and then to get on with one's work.

But what can you do if you are seized with a violent emotion while you are in the street? You cannot shake it off if you keep on walking, so you will have to stop. Stop in front of a shop, for instance, and pretend to be looking at something in the window, so that the passers-by will not notice anything out of the ordinary, and try to solve the problem that has put you into such a state. Merely interrupting your movement will enable you to steer your thoughts in a different direction.

Blow away the clouds

When you are in a bad mood or feeling sad or worried, it means that a cloud is crossing your sky. When this happens, instead of feeding it and making it even bigger by dwelling on all that is troubling you, meditate and try to blow it away. If you succeed, you will see that the sun, God, is still there, that he was only hidden from you by your own clouds.

And if you can do this on a small scale, why not learn to do it on a large scale? Once you know how to get rid of your own clouds, you can try to scatter the collective clouds that weigh so heavily on the earth.

Once you have sown one grain of wheat and seen the beautiful ears it produces, you can sow a whole field with thousands of similar grains, for you know in advance that they will also produce ears of wheat. And this applies to your spiritual work, too: once you have achieved the results you desired for yourself, you can be sure that you are also capable of helping the whole of humanity.

Have a bath

Water has the property of absorbing everything. It absorbs both good and evil, and this is why, when you are in a state of great wonder or delight, you should not wash: above all, you should not have a bath. But if you have a bath when you are feeling unhappy, it will do you a lot of good: the water will wash away your sadness.

Set a limit to your problem

If you have a migraine headache or an upset stomach, for example, or if you are pursued by grief or evil thoughts, it helps to go out for a walk. As you walk, say to yourself: 'When I get to that tree—or lamp-post, gate, wall—I shall be feeling better.' Walk towards the landmark you have chosen in the conviction that you really will be rid of your problem and that by the time you reach it you will feel better. If the improvement is too slight, pick another landmark farther on, and repeat to yourself with insistence that by the time you reach it your problem will have completely disappeared. Keep doing this until you feel a real improvement.

The power of love

When you are feeling cross and irritable or discouraged, instead of giving way to despair or making a nuisance of yourself, stay quietly at home, telling yourself: 'I've let myself get cold; I must warm up.' Then take a few deep breaths, do something, any little gesture, with love and send a loving thought to the whole universe, for love is true warmth. You will find that by sending out waves of love you have opened the floodgates of your heart and that the water has begun to flow. Let it flow and do its work: it will purify everything within you.

The power of words

Initiation teaches disciples how to use words in such a way as to release the forces of nature. Words have great power, but we still do not know how to use them or even pronounce them correctly.

When you are cold or feel neglected, when you have the impression that nobody loves you, say the word 'love' once, twice, ten times, each time a little differently; in this way you will be setting in motion and surrounding yourself with cosmic powers of love, and it will be impossible for you to go on feeling alone or abandoned.

When you are utterly in the dark and feel as though you have fallen into a deep pit, repeat the words 'wisdom' and 'light' until they throb and sing in every cell of your body. Then everything will become clear to you.

When you feel tormented, hemmed in, and anxious, repeat the word 'freedom'.

And you can also repeat the words 'beauty', 'truth', 'strength', 'health', and 'harmony'. You might say that that does not amount to much, but if you learn how to utter each word with intensity and conviction, it gathers more and more power as you say it and influences the matter of your being.

The power of song

The songs we sing here in the Brotherhood have a beneficial influence on you, even when you do not actually sing them. The simple fact of having them in your mind does you good because they fill you with their vibrations.

When you do not quite know where you stand or where you are going, when your ideas are all confused, sing *Misli, pravo misli*—'Think rightly', and you will begin to see your way more clearly. When you feel that nobody loves you any more, sing *Bog e lubov*—'God is love', and what more could you need? God will never abandon you. If you are tired or ill, sing *Sila zdrave e bogatsvo*—'Strength and health are wealth', and everything, the very walls and ceiling, will begin to quiver and vibrate, and you will find yourself on your feet again, full of ardour. And if you have lost your zest for life, if everything seems tasteless and without joy, say, *Krassiv e jivota* —'Life is beautiful!'[4]

You have a treasure house of possibilities there, an arsenal of magic weapons, and you must learn to use them.

How to combat the forces of evil

If you are distressed or tempted, it means that you are being attacked by evil spirits. When this happens, you must not go sallying forth to give battle: if you leave the safety of your inner fortress, you will certainly be wounded, because you have no shield or armour or weapon. On the contrary, you must enter more deeply into yourself.

Instead of going out to fight enemies that are too powerful for you, run away from them and take refuge inside yourself. If you try to pit yourself against them you will only become more and more irritable, impatient, and tense. So do not engage in battle; be content to retreat to your inner fortress. Try not to think about the enemy or worry about what he might be doing; just wait. Stay safely in your secret place and think of the Lord, and after a little while you will find that your enemies have gone away. And what should you do if you find that they have not gone away, that they are still there? Well, at least you will have armed yourself with light, strength, and wisdom while you were in your inner fortress and will be in a better position to attack them with real weapons.

Let your enemies rant and rave as much as they like. Stay where you are, do not move and do not worry about them, and above all do not try to pit yourself against them until you are

4.These are all titles from the collection of mystical songs of the Universal White Brotherhood.

fully armed and ready for combat. Instead of struggling, wasting a lot of energy and exhausting yourself, leave them alone and climb up into that secret refuge on high where God dwells in you. God does not live within reach of his enemies. He who is true strength and power dwells in the deepest recesses of our being, and that is where we must go to look for him. When you are being threatened, therefore, leave whatever you are doing, recollect yourself, and think of the divine spirit who dwells in you. When you reach him with your thought, he will tell you: 'Come to me, child; your enemies are pursuing you, but you will be safe with me.'

Suppose that you are invaded by negative thoughts or feelings and in spite of all your efforts you cannot drive them away: what should you do? Adopt the attitude of an observer. Look calmly at the negative forces and entities, and observe how they manifest themselves and the tricks they are up to. When you do this you are putting yourself above them and they dislike that. When they feel that someone is watching them it makes them uneasy, and if you then flash a beam of light on them they will scatter and disappear, for they hate light. They may come back— in fact, they will certainly come back until you change your ingrained patterns—but when they do you can use the same tactics: look at them steadily and project a ray of light on them, and in the long run you will get rid of them. The secret is to get to a higher level than theirs and stay there.

Prayer against evil spirits

In the name of divine love, changeless and eternal,
In the name of divine wisdom, changeless and eternal,
In which we move and have our being;
And in the name of the magic living word,
May all evil and every thought inspired by the devil
be dispelled and annihilated.

The difficulties of life

Be prepared for difficult periods

Our consciousness is sometimes full of light and sometimes
in darkness, sometimes brimful and sometimes empty, for we are
subject to the same fluctuations as nature. This is why it is
important to know when each phenomenon is going to recur. If
you cannot see that the pendulum is about to swing back to a
difficult period, you may commit yourself unwisely to such or
such an undertaking, and then when the time comes, you find
yourself in the doldrums, without inspiration or joy. You could
have avoided this if you had realized in advance that the dark
days were about to begin and that you would be feeling weak
and dejected. All our faults are committed in darkness when our
consciousness is obscured. So learn to sense the advent of those
moments, and when they come do not undertake anything
important.

Do not run from difficulties

If you try to avoid making an effort or facing up to difficulties, you will inevitably encounter even greater difficulties
than those you avoided. Instead of trying to run away from
problems, you have to try to solve them, otherwise you will only
make the situation worse for yourself. A change of scenery will
only be beneficial if you have already solved the problem that
faced you. If you try to wriggle out of doing your duty and make
things easier for yourself, it shows that you do not know the
severe laws that govern human destiny. The invisible world will
simply say, 'You failed to resolve any of your problems then, so
do it now!' So instead of running from your difficulties, try to
understand the reason for them and do what has to be done. Once
you sense that you have done all you had to do, then you can go

wherever you like, even to hell, in perfect peace of mind, because the angels prepare the way for those who have accomplished the whole of their duty.

Accept your trials with gratitude

You may well follow a spiritual teaching and live in the light, but this does not mean that you will never have an accident or a mishap of some kind. Nobody is immune from problems simply because they are in an initiatic school. If you want to be sure that nothing bad can ever happen to you, you must pay off all your debts left over from the past. If you still have unpaid debts, whether you follow a spiritual teaching or not, whether you live in the light or not, you are going to have to settle them. You say that you follow this divine teaching—true. You say that you live in the light—true. That you never do any harm, only good—true again. But you must realize that the good you do will bear fruit only in the future, not in the immediate present. So when you are faced with trials and tribulations, you must accept them, saying, 'Lord, none of this can obliterate the work I have already done with light. So much the better if I am having problems: it means that I am becoming freer, and that is wonderful. Now that I know the reason for my trials I shall not rebel against them any more; I no longer ask to be spared.'

Some good can always come out of evil

Whatever the circumstances and events of your life, you must always try to see the good side. When you are confronted with evil in the form of difficulties, illness, or accidents, therefore, always try to remember that good can come out of it: this puts everything in perspective. Tell yourself: 'Why not put up with a few little misfortunes in order to gain great good fortune?' Many people have achieved magnificent things thanks to their misfortunes. If they had never had certain difficulties they would never have accomplished anything out of the ordinary, anything great, noble, or divine. So scrutinize carefully everything that happens to you and ask yourself why the invisible world has sent you a particular difficulty or failure, and what it expects of you.

If you get into the habit of taking a second look at obstacles or events that seem at first sight to be misfortunes, you will see that you can always find some good in them. Happiness is often lying in wait in the most unexpected places. You would like it to conform to your own preconceived ideas, but it never does. But do not let that discourage you; you are not alone. There are hosts of invisible beings who are constantly thinking of you and instructing and advising you.

Chapter Six

Methods of Purification[1]

1.See *Complete Works*, vol. 7, for a fuller treatment of purity.

Fasting

Fasting is beneficial for health

All initiates recommend fasting, because they know that it purifies one's organism and that health is based on purity.

If you never fast, the cells of your stomach and other organs get into the habit of counting on you, their master: they know that you will always give them all they need and they grow lazy. Also, as you always give them too much food, they cannot absorb it all, and some of it stagnates in the tissues and begins to ferment and rot. Whereas, when you fast and your cells discover that they are not being given anything to eat, they learn to be wiser, more economical, and more active in order to survive on their reserves. When this is the case, fermentation is no longer a problem.

If you never fast you are heading for a very dangerous situation in the future, for your cells will become passive, lazy, and weak. Of course, too long a fast can weaken the organism and even cause death. But if you know how long to fast, and the conditions in which to do so, and if you set about it in the right spirit, then the benefits for your health can be immense.

The weekly fast

It is excellent to get into the habit of fasting for twenty-four hours once a week. During those twenty-four hours you can drink some very hot, boiled water, but nothing else, and take the opportunity to do some spiritual work: try to put yourself in touch with the most luminous entities, and listen to some music or read something that inspires you and helps to purify your thoughts and feelings.

Fasting and the spiritual life

1. Fasting strengthens one's mental faculties

The beneficial effects of fasting are not limited to physical health. Initiates fast when they want to help or save someone who is experiencing difficulties, because in this way they accumulate spiritual energies which they can then pass on to those who need them. For this reason initiates often deprive themselves of food in order to help their family and friends.

2. Fasting drives out harmful entities

By fasting we can drive out the harmful entities which come and take shelter in us. As soon as we begin to fast, on the very first day, they start complaining, 'Our master has become so cruel; he refuses to give us anything to eat!' and many of them go off to look for someone else who will nourish them. Of course, there are others that cling to you more stubbornly: they will not leave until the second or third day, or even later. But as each day goes by, more and more of these noxious entities abandon us and we feel more and more peaceful, lucid, and free. When Jesus' disciples asked him how to drive out devils, he replied: by prayer and fasting. There is no other way. If you never fast, the inferior entities within you will become stronger and stronger until they are so powerful that they will destroy you completely.

Ending a fast

After fasting for several days you must be careful not to begin eating normally at once, otherwise you can give yourself some very serious problems and even kill yourself.

On the first day it is good to drink several cups of light vegetable broth; the second day you can have some soup and rusks or toast, and on the third day you can begin to eat normal meals of light food, but without taking too much. If you do this you will be in no danger, and after a fast like that you will experience new, subtle sensations: you will feel rejuvenated and cleansed, because the wastes and impurities that had been clogging your organism have disappeared and been burned away.

Perspiration

The chemical composition of perspiration is exactly the same as that of urine, the only difference being that perspiration is more diluted. When you sweat, your skin is doing the same work as the kidneys: by eliminating toxins through the pores, it is cleansing and purifying you. There are various ways of promoting perspiration, and the one I recommend is to drink hot water. Boil the water and drink it as hot as possible. By a process of osmosis, hot water penetrates and dilates the ducts of the body and then, by capillary attraction, rises to the surface and exits through the pores of the skin. When you induce perspiration in this way you feel renewed, purified, and strengthened.

Perspiration is essential for good health. If you feel feverish and have a cold coming on, for instance, you can cure it by drinking several cups of boiling hot water and inducing perspiration, thereby helping to eliminate the toxins in your system.

The four elements

All human beings have certain noxious germs in their subconscious, and these germs have no difficulty in finding suitable conditions in which to grow and thrive. Eventually, they can become a real handicap in the lives of their hosts. This is why, when disciples are already well advanced on the path of evolution, they are given the task of penetrating into the depths of their own subconscious and, with the help of the angels of the four elements—the angels of earth, water, air, and fire—of getting rid of those germs. They either burn them with the help of fire, scatter them with the help of the wind, drown them in water, or bury them in the earth. In this way they achieve total freedom.

It is important to know the particular role of each of the four elements.

Earth

The earth has the particular property of absorbing our impurities. It acts as a magnet to attract and soak up every kind of dirt and impurity, and sends it all down to be processed and transformed in its underground laboratories. You can see for yourselves how the earth absorbs and transforms all our wastes and gives them back to us in the form of flowers and succulent fruits. This is why, whenever you feel weighed down by problems, anxieties or impurities, I advise you to give them to the earth. Make a little hole in the ground and put your fingers into it, and then talk to the earth as to an intelligent, living being, asking it to relieve you of all that torments you. Say, 'O Earth, my mother, you have given me all the elements of my physical body, and I thank you for them. And now I beg you to take away all the impurities that have been accumulating in me for years, and to send them to your marvellous workshops and laboratories. Transform them into the purest elements and then send them back to me, so that I may accomplish my work in the world.' To conclude, you can recite the cabbalistic formula I have already given you: Taro-Tora-Rota-Tarota-Rotaro.

Water

Water is an element that is particularly effective for purification, for it has the capacity to extract and absorb elements from whatever it flows through. On the etheric plane, also, water has this same capacity to retain and absorb etheric elements, and this is why initiates work with water in order to wash away psychic impurities. They pronounce certain formulas and use certain substances in order to exalt the water and enhance its power.

But water can only help you to obtain true purification if you use it as a medium through which to reach the spiritual, cosmic water that is above and beyond psychic water. Until you make contact with that water, you can never completely wash away the layers of impure fluids that cover you.

1. How to take a bath

Most people never think that when they wash their physical body they could at the same time do something to purify their etheric and astral bodies. The etheric and astral regions contain impurities which are very difficult to get rid of; in fact, those of the astral plane are more potent, more offensive, and more noxious than those of any other plane. However, water is capable of washing away these impurities if it is vivified in advance. To do this you must prepare some salt (as you probably know, salt has a significant role in many religious ceremonies) in the following way: in the morning, you light some candles and burn incense and then, taking some salt, you say a few words to dedicate it to absolute purity, to the Supreme Mother and the

Cosmic Spirit, and to ask heavenly intelligences to bless it and give it the virtue of purification.

Before getting into the bath, sprinkle the consecrated salt into the water and say a few words so that the power it contains sanctifies the water; then you address the Supreme Mother in these words: 'O divine Mother, how I admire this water that reflects your divine countenance. I beg you to sanctify it so that it may wash away all my impurities, sickness, and weaknesses and make me better able to serve my Heavenly Father.' After that you touch the water with your hand and speak to the creatures that inhabit it, saying, 'O beautiful, pure, transparent nymphs, bid me welcome, open your arms to me and wash away everything in me that is not in harmony with heaven.' While you are saying this, touch the water very lovingly.

Water is inhabited by many invisible entities which are very pure and beautiful, and by entering into contact with water, you communicate with these sensitive beings, and they will be ready to help you if you have an attitude of love and respect. Before getting into your bath, take from it a jugful of the blessed water to pour over yourself when you have finished washing, and as you get into the water, speak to it: tell it how beautiful it is and how full of admiration and wonder you are. Wash yourself with soap three times. If your faith and love are strong, a bath like this will benefit you tremendously; it all depends on your faith and love.

2. Using water mentally

Of course, it can happen that you feel the need to purify yourself when it is not possible to have a bath or wash with water. That does not matter: you can still take a spiritual bath and wash yourself mentally. Imagine the coolness of water on your skin, the sensation of a shower of water pouring over you and washing away all your impurities. A spiritual bath can really truly cleanse you because, after all, water is not primarily physical. True water can only be found within the human heart; this was the water Jesus was speaking about when he said, 'From his heart will flow rivers of living water.' Physical water is simply the medium through which we make contact with spiritual water.

3. How to wash away a black mood

You all know what it is to be in the grip of a grief or sorrow that you are unable to shake off. When this happens, it is a great help to watch and listen to running water—even if it is only water from a tap. After a few moments you will feel a certain relief. What has happened? The running water has had a cleansing, soothing effect on the solar plexus and washed away whatever was upsetting it.

Another helpful method is to plunge your hands into either hot or cold water. In a very few minutes you will feel lighter; the burden will be lifted.

Or you can wash your hands with soap, once, twice—as many as ten times if you like. And while you are washing your physical hands, you can also mentally wash your etheric hands.

4. How to magnetize water

When your hands have been washed, they can become conductors of celestial energies, and you can use them, for example, to inject these energies into a glass of water before drinking it. Take a glass of pure water (preferably spring water or water from a mountain lake) in your left hand and dip the first three fingers (thumb, index, and middle fingers) of the right hand into it while concentrating on love, wisdom, and truth, so as to impregnate the water with these three virtues. Then, as you drink the water, say to yourself: 'For the love that heals, the wisdom that gives light, the truth that sets us free.'

Air[1]

1. An exercise with the Angel of Air

On a windy day, go out and walk in the wind and ask the Angel of Air to blow away all your cares and impurities.

2. Expose your body to the air

If you can find a sheltered spot where you can be alone, expose your naked body to the air and imagine it blowing through you and taking all your impurities with it.

Fire[2]

Fire represents the borderline between the physical and the etheric worlds; it is a door opening on to the world above. This is why fire makes the divine world more accessible to us. Initiates have adopted the custom of lighting a flame before performing a ceremony or gesture of any importance because they know that only fire has the power to introduce them into the subtle regions on high and allow their thought and their voice to be heard.

1. Exercise in front of an open fire

You have all watched a wood fire blazing in a hearth, but have you ever wondered exactly what happens to make all those dead, dark, twisted logs and branches so bright and beautiful? Isn't it miraculous to see something that was so black being transformed into something so luminous? But you can do the same: whether you are at home in front of your own fireplace, or here, gathered round the fire at the Bonfin, you can use your imagination to burn your own dead branches—that is, all your atavistic, instinctive tendencies. All that useless dead wood—into the fire with it! Fire is capable of converting everything into

---

1.See also the section on breathing in chap. 2.
2.For a fuller discussion of fire and of the sun, see chap. 9.

heat and light, and it is you who stand to gain; otherwise, what use would all those dead branches be to you? They can give you neither warmth nor light because you lack the power to transform them. Give them to the fire, and it will give them back to you in the form of light and heat.

2. Exercise with a lighted candle

This exercise should be done in a quiet room. Before lighting a candle, begin by preparing yourself quietly, in a spirit of recollection. Then dedicate your candle to an idea or an entity: the Supreme Mother, for example, or the Heavenly Father, the Holy Spirit, the Universal Soul, the Archangel Mikhaël...

Once your candle is alight, the four elements are present: fire; air—without which fire cannot burn; earth—represented by the solid part of the candle; and water—represented by the melted wax. Look at the flame and reflect that you are looking at the greatest mystery of nature; look at it as though you were seeing it for the first time. Like a drop of sea water, which contains all the properties of the entire ocean, this flame is a drop of the cosmic ocean, of universal fire. It is a focal point radiating light, heat, and life; it is your link with the immensity of cosmic life.

When you feel that you have established a bond between yourself and the flame, bend over it, open your mouth and breathe in three times. Hold your breath for a moment before breathing out again. The exercise should be done four times, once for each of the four bodies—physical, etheric, astral, and mental:

– For the physical body, in order to awaken the forces dormant within it and protect it from fire;

– For the etheric body, in order to impregnate it with the vibrations of the flame;

– For the astral body, so that peace and harmony may dwell in your heart;

– For the mental body, so that your thoughts may be full of light.

When you bow your head over the flame and breathe in, you are breathing in the life that rises to the tip of the flame, and you can feel it strengthening you.

When the Angel of Fire sees your admiration for this living flame, he will love you and help you, and if you succeed in synchronizing your vibrations with those of fire, you will escape destruction when the whole world goes up in flames.

When you do this exercise you must pray and concentrate your thought on your desire that the flame shall come to dwell in you. Speak to it, saying, 'Beloved flame, symbol of the Holy Spirit, symbol of cosmic fire, symbol of the sun, enter into me and impregnate all the cells of my body so that one day the Holy Spirit may come and dwell within me.'

Prayer to the angels of the four elements

Lord God almighty, creator of heaven and earth,
most clement and merciful Father,
send me your four angels:
The Angel of Earth, the Angel of Water,
The Angel of Air and the Angel of Fire,
That your will may be made manifest in me.

May the Angel of Earth take all the wastes of my physical body and give them to the earth, that she may absorb them and send them back to me in the form of health and purity. May he cleanse my whole body so that life may flow abundantly through my veins and arteries. May my whole being be free, light, and unburdened, so that the kingdom of God and his righteousness may be established on earth and the golden age dawn among men.

May the Angel of Water wash all stains from my heart. May selfless love dwell in my heart, bringing me happiness, joy, and bliss. May my heart be pure, transparent, and crystal clear, so that the kingdom of God and his righteousness may be established on earth and the golden age dawn among men.

May the Angel of Air purify my intellect with an influx of wisdom and light. May my thought become lucid, keen, and radiant, so that the kingdom of God and his righteousness may be established on earth and the golden age dawn among men.

And may the Angel of Fire, who is none other than the Angel of the Sun, sanctify my soul and my spirit. May absolute truth penetrate my whole being. May my soul and my spirit know eternal life and be a dwelling for divine creative omnipotence, so that the kingdom of God and his righteousness may be established on earth and the golden age dawn among men.

Amen, amen, amen.

So be it, so be it, so be it.

Purity must be sought on a higher level

If you really want to attain purity, you must move to a higher plane and communicate with heaven. On the lower levels you will find only the dregs: filth, impurities, and slime—all the toxic, heavy elements that sink to the bottom. If you want to enjoy all that is transparent, crystalline, and etheric you will have to look for it on high. Those who make a constant effort to rise to a higher level, to keep rising until they reach God himself, attain purity even if they are not specifically looking for it. The effort that it takes to transcend one's limitations and rise to ever greater heights cleanses and purifies all one's subtle bodies.

If you send something to the cleaners to be dry-cleaned or washed or bleached, it is put into a steam bath or soaked in a tub of hot water or cleaning fluid. This is what happens to us, too. When we ally ourselves with God, we are already, by means of our subtle bodies, immersed in a different atmosphere, in other currents and vibrations which influence us and wipe out all our stains and transgressions. Yes, there are all kinds of 'washing machines' on high, and when you expose yourself to their powerful jets of 'steam', they purify you. If you keep a handkerchief in a box which has had scent in it, after a few days you will find that it is impregnated with the scent. Similarly, if you frequent regions rich in light and perfume, you will become impregnated with their quintessences; your whole being will be luminous and fragrant, and everybody will begin to notice that something divine emanates from you; wherever you go, you will take with you that atmosphere of beauty, purity, and light. Believe me, this is an absolute reality.

Never forget, therefore, that there is only one way to purify yourself and become lucid and clear-sighted, and that is to move to a higher level, to climb and keep climbing, always higher and higher. It is on high that the best ideas and desires are to be found; all that is best and most beautiful belongs to the world above, where everything is luminous and fragrant.

Chapter Seven

Human Relations

Debts of gratitude

1. Debts to family, society, and race

Our parents give us our physical body, life (although, of course, it is not they who create the life they give us), food, clothes, housing, and education. And all these things add up to a considerable debt for which they are entitled to claim repayment. Many young people refuse to acknowledge this. They are critical and antagonistic towards their parents; many detest them, even. This is highly unjust. Their parents have loved them and suffered for them, they have fed, clothed, and protected them, looked after them when they were ill and given them an education. Man's first debt, therefore, is to his parents.

But human beings also have a debt to the society or nation to which they belong, because it has given them a rich heritage of culture and civilization, with museums, libraries, laboratories, and theatres. It provides them with means of transport—trains, ships, and planes; doctors to take care of their health; teachers for their instruction; an army and even a police force for their protection.

They also owe something to their race, for it gives them not only the colour of their skin but their whole physical and psychic structure, a particular mentality.

*But it does not end there: humanity also has a debt to the planet Earth which bears and nourishes us, to the solar system (because it is thanks to the sun and the other planets that we receive what we need to vivify and sustain us), to the entire universe, and, finally, to God himself.

Most human beings are content to take; they are not aware of the tremendous debts they incur. But disciples are conscious of their debts and do their best to pay them. This is why, first and foremost, they love their parents and try to repay their debt to them by helping them and doing them good. They also give something to society, to their country, and to humanity as a whole, to the solar system, the cosmos, and God himself. Through their activities and all their thoughts and feelings, they never cease to give something good to them all, and nature sees this and recognizes them as intelligent beings.

2. Disciples are indebted to their master

As disciples, you also have a tremendous debt to your master. If you ask, 'How much should we give him?' the answer is 'Nothing'. He does not ask anything of you, but one day you will have to do for others what he does for you; one day you will have to show the same abnegation, magnanimity, and love to others; that is how you will pay your debt. Justice must reign in every area. I, too, have received immense gifts from God. The Lord has always taken care of me—and still does. He has illuminated and instructed me, and I am now in debt to him for all those graces and blessings, for all that abundance of love showered on me day and night. How am I paying my debts? By working for him, by preparing the ground for the coming of his kingdom. So what about you? Do you really think you are going to get away without paying? Oh, how ignorant you are! Make no mistake about it, you are going to have to pay, too!

Relationships of affection

1. Love without asking to be loved in return

If you are always waiting to be loved you will never be happy, because you are relying on something that will always be uncertain. You may be loved today, but who can tell what will happen tomorrow? Never rely on the love of others. It may be given to you, of course; in fact, you may never be without it, and when it comes it is a very welcome gift—but even then you should not rely on it.

This is why I say that if you want to be happy, stop asking to be loved by others; be content to love them, ceaselessly and unfailingly, day and night. If you do this, your happiness too will be unfailing. Perhaps one day someone will love you with a great love. Why not? It could happen! But do not count on it. That is how I have resolved the problem: I count only on my own love for others. I want to love, and if others do not want to, that is their business; they will be unhappy but I am happy!

2. Relationship between parents and children

Most parents firmly believe that it is they who created their own children and that they are entitled to behave as they please towards them. No, parents must understand that all they have done is build their child's house, his physical body. It was not they who created his soul: that comes from somewhere else, from very far away. A child is sent to study with his parents, just as a student may be sent to study in a foreign country. His family is the 'boarding school' which provides him with room and board, instruction and education. A child comes from a distant country, and his parents in this life are his guardians and tutors; their work is to nourish and educate him until his heavenly Father comes to claim him.

When a child is sent as a boarder with another family, everybody knows it will not last for ever; sooner or later his parents will come to take him home. They will ask how much they owe to those who have been looking after him, and if he has been well cared for, they will pay generously. Similarly, parents must realize that their children have been 'lent' to them by God, and that they must treat them well, so that when they go back to their Father, they will be able to tell him about the love and care they received.

3. Relationships between men and women

a) Love

Human beings will never solve the problem of love until they change their attitude towards each other. The cause of every deviation or exaggeration in this area is the fact that men have never learned the right attitude towards women, and women have never learned the right attitude towards men. If a man looks on women simply as females, as objects of pleasure, he will behave accordingly and give expression to all his basest tendencies. But if he sees women as divinities, his behaviour will be very different. Jesus said, 'As you have believed, so let it be done for you.' It is your attitude, the way you perceive people and things, that determine what they are: it is a question of magic. But nobody has ever explained this. It is no use hoping to change the form that your love takes if you fail to change your attitude towards the object of your love. It is very difficult to change one's way of loving, but if you change your conception of someone it will automatically change you as well as your feelings and tendencies and the way you manifest yourself.

This is what I do: I look on woman as a divinity. You probably feel inclined to pity me: 'Poor fellow; you are a long way from the truth! If you only knew what women were really like!' Do you really believe that I do not know? But I refuse to dwell on that; I am not interested in knowing what women are like or what they are capable of on the lowest levels. It is the reality of woman on the highest, heavenly levels that interests me: her reality as a divine spark, a representative of the Supreme Mother, a manifestation of poetry and beauty. And you, too, should change your conceptions. Men must change their opinion of women, and women of men, otherwise the paths of evolution will be closed to them and they will never make progress. Women must also see man as a divinity. There is a great difference in the attitude of someone who sees human beings as a conglomeration of molecules and atoms, and someone who sees them as souls and spirits.

If a man and woman want to manifest true love and experience true happiness and freedom, they must always see each other as representatives of the heavenly Father and the divine Mother. Otherwise, when the man embraces his beloved, he will, at the same time, embrace her weaknesses and limitations; he will never attain anything higher or greater or purer, and their love will not last. So now there must be another, a new understanding: let man see his wife as the representative of the divine Mother, and let the woman see her husband as an aspect of the heavenly Father. If they think of each other in these terms, they will both be in touch with something of a higher order, and both will be something more than themselves; when they are in each other's arms they will both be holding in their embrace, in their heart and soul, something of immensity, and rays and currents of a subtler nature will flow from that immensity. Then the angels and devas and spirits of nature will bring gifts of strength and joy to these two beings who are expressing themselves in the most beautiful language of creation, the language of love, limitless love.

b) The daily life of a couple

Let us look at a married couple and see what happens in their everyday life together.

Every morning the husband leaves for work: 'Goodbye, darling... Goodbye,' and they give each other a perfunctory kiss, both of them thinking of something else. As soon as the door has closed behind her husband, the woman starts grumbling to herself: 'That so-and-so! Why was I fool enough to marry him? He's nothing but a lazy, good-for-nothing! When I think of how successful the man next door is... Look at his car, and the furs and jewellery he buys for his wife... Oh, I could scream!' And she mopes and moans and swears to tell her husband what she thinks of him: 'I won't put up with it a minute longer. When he comes home I'll have it out with him. This time he's really going to be in for a shock!' And she spends the rest of the day in a fury, preparing for battle and poisoning herself with negativity.

And he? What is going through his head? 'Ah, the b...! Whatever made me think I loved her? The stupid, empty-headed nobody! When I think of the hours she spends in the shops with that horrible little dog of hers, or stuffing herself with cakes at tea parties! She never does anything useful, whereas I spend my days working for a pittance in this filthy, noisy factory. I won't stand for it any longer!' And in his imagination he shakes his fist at her and prepares for the fight he is going to have when he gets home.

So they spend the day grumbling and the evening tearing each other apart... And the next day the same scenario begins all over again!

But now let me show you what it will be like when men and women decide to change their attitude.

In the morning, before he goes to work, they will kiss, but tenderly, with real warmth; and when he has left the house, she will begin to think to herself: 'Ah, the poor darling, when I think of the sacrifices he makes for my sake! It's incredible that he should have married someone like me... He's so upright and honest, so noble! And so loving... when I remember his kisses! He spends his whole day slaving away in that dusty, noisy factory, just to be able to bring me some money, whereas I'm as free as air: I can go out for a walk or have a rest when I feel like it, whereas he never gets a break. Ah, I know what I'll do: I'll cook his favourite dinner for him tonight...' And all day long she thinks of him and is happy. And he, for his part, thinks to himself: 'Why did she marry me? The poor darling is a slave; she spends her days cleaning the house and looking after the children, washing them and preparing meals. She never has a minute to herself... never has time to go out for a walk. She's alone all day at home, while I go to the pub and have a good chat with my pals! Oh, she's a wonderful woman; I'm going to show her how I feel about her.' And he buys her a bunch of flowers or a little present to surprise her with, and when he gets home they are so glad to be together they fall into each others arms, kissing and hugging with such love!

The real difference between these two couples lies in their heads, in their different points of view, in the different attitudes they have towards each other. And it is so easy to change one's point of view. To change oneself is not at all easy; but if you begin by changing your point of view, everything else changes too.

Relationships of hostility

1. The bonds of hatred are as strong as those of love

When you detest someone, it is exactly as though you loved them: you forge a bond between you. Hatred is as powerful as love. If you want to free yourself from someone and never see them again, do not hate them: be indifferent to them. If you hate them you will be binding yourself to them with chains that can never be broken; they will always be with you, and you will be obliged to deal with them for years and years. Hatred is a force that binds us to those we hate. So is love. But the bonds of love are, of course, different. Love brings certain things with it, and hatred brings others, but just as surely and just as powerfully as love.

2. Love as a weapon of defence

The best way to defend yourself against your enemies is to love them. If you hate or despise or detest them, you rend the fabric of your aura, and all their negative, noxious aspects flood into you through those rents. Once the evil and hatred of your enemies invade your aura, they begin to destroy you.

This is why Jesus said, 'Love your enemies.' Jesus knew these great laws; he knew that if you detested someone you became vulnerable. To defend yourself, you must retreat into the impregnable fortress of love. To love one's enemies is one of the most difficult things anyone can do, but it is the only way to defend oneself against them.

3. Use injuries as a spiritual incentive

At the least little insult or injury, your lower nature tells you to avenge yourself: 'Hit him; break his jaw for him and teach him a lesson!' and you scramble to do its bidding. But your higher nature says, 'Don't let it bother you; that's the way it is. And you can use that insult and transform and sublimate it; you're an alchemist, and you can turn it into gold!' And there you are, launching into the adventure of this great work from which you stand to gain so much. When someone injures you or blames you unjustly, your higher self says, 'Why waste hours moaning about it instead of working? You should be grateful to heaven; that person was sent specially to give you this opportunity to grow, and all you do is sit there feeling sorry for yourself! Don't be so stupid.' Disciples refuse to follow the advice of their lower nature; they refuse to take offence at everything and be touchy, weak and sentimental, capricious, unbalanced, unorganized, and chaotic. This is why they always try to discover the positive side of everything that happens to them and to work with it.

4. How to forgive

Those who are spiritually weak and poor are incapable of forgiveness; they will always seek revenge. In order to forgive someone who has done you a wrong, you have to be big-hearted, rich, strong, and luminous. You have to say to yourself: 'I have to forgive the poor wretch, he doesn't know the harm he is doing to himself by injuring me. The laws of justice are implacable; he's going to have to suffer to atone for the wrong he is doing. It's all right for me: even if I'm being victimized I have the privilege of working for good, for the kingdom of God, for the light.' If you see things this way and think of the splendour in which you live because you have chosen the path of good, compared to the distress and obscurity that haunts those who are unjust and evil, you will be seized by feelings of pity, tolerance, and love. In this way you will have no difficulty in achieving an attitude of generosity and forgiveness, which cannot be achieved in any other way.

Perhaps some of you will say, 'It seems to me that this attitude is very like that of the Pharisee who thanked God that he was not like other men—especially not like the tax collector kneeling at the back of the Temple. It's an attitude of pride!' No, not at all. The Pharisee took pride in the fact that he fasted twice a week and gave away tithes of all he possessed, and he despised the tax collector who may well have been a better man. The attitude I am talking about is quite different. I am saying that if in the face of calumny or injustice you think of all the marvellous gifts that God has given you, whereas your enemy is deprived of them, you will realize that you are privileged. Perhaps for the moment they have the whip hand and seem to have got the better of you. And yet it is they who are to be pitied, not you; for someone who does wrong is always to be pitied, and, in one way or another, divine justice will punish them. So you see that the attitude I am advising is quite different from the

Pharisee's. It is in this sense that we must understand Jesus' words: 'Father, forgive them for they do not know what they do.'

5. Vanquish your enemies by rising above them

People think that they can vanquish or rid themselves of their enemies by constantly speaking ill of them, but they are very mistaken. You will never get the better of an enemy by taking their portrait with you wherever you go: sooner or later it is they who will be victorious. You cannot vanquish the vindictive with vindictiveness, slanderers with slander, those who are jealous or angry with your own jealousy and anger. If you use their weapons you sink to their level and identify with them; you put yourself into the same category.

To protect yourself and become invulnerable, you have to move to another level and cease sharing the same wavelength, the same weaknesses and the same emanations as your enemy, for if they are stronger than you are, they will contaminate you. You must move up to a higher level, to nobler, purer, more luminous regions. Once you are on higher ground, thanks to your will-power and your prayers and meditations, your enemy can no longer reach you: your vibrations are not the same. When you are protected by barricades of light and love and heavenly power, not only can vindictiveness not touch you but it will rebound on to its authors and bite and crush them.

This is how sages, initiates, and the great masters overcome their enemies. They live such radiant lives of purity, nobility, and integrity that, sooner or later, all those who attack them so relentlessly come to grief from the backlash of their own vindictiveness. But if you are just as weak, evil, and sensual as they are, there will be no backlash. On the contrary, it is you who will receive the full force of the filth they aim at you. But if you put yourself on a much higher level, the life you lead will itself be your protection; everything negative and evil will glance off it and fall back on those who threw it. If you really want to be safe and protect yourself from whatever anyone may say or do to wound you, therefore, you must change your way of life, tune yourself to a different wavelength, climb to a higher plane where you will be invulnerable.

Two ways of helping mankind

1. Send thoughts of light to heads of State

Most people fling nothing but criticism and abuse at those who bear the burden of government. In fact, newspapers, cabarets, and reviews make a point of laughing at political leaders and making them look ridiculous in order to amuse the public. The result is that these unfortunate men and women are influenced by such a burden of negative, wounding thoughts that they adopt the wrong policies for the country, and, of course, the whole population suffers from their mistakes. If you want to help your country, you must touch the person in charge with thoughts of light, so that he or she may always be well inspired. You cannot help a whole country directly; it is too big. It is enough— and it is far easier—to help one person, just one. And this one person, in turn, will help everybody else, for much depends on the leader. If he or she can promote just laws in the areas of public health, housing, and education, the whole population will benefit, all because one person was well inspired.

2. See humanity as a single being

People have the impression that there is nothing they can do to help or improve humanity as a whole. They say, 'There are just too many people; it's an impossible task.' Well, it might seem impossible—it is certainly gigantic—but if you learn certain methods, you will see that all of a sudden it becomes possible.

Try to imagine, for instance, that the whole of humankind is condensed into a single being, standing there by your side, and you hold the hand of this being and give them quantities of light and love. When you do this, some minute particles go out from your soul, and the love you give this one being reflects on every human being in the world, and they begin to conceive nobler thoughts and desires in their hearts.

If hundreds and thousands of people on earth did this exercise, you would see the breath of a new, divine spirit in humanity, and without knowing how or why, they would wake up one day to find themselves completely transformed.

Chapter Eight

Our Relations with Nature

The whole of nature is alive

When initiates open their door in the morning, before doing anything else, they salute nature: the trees, the sky, and the sun, the day itself and the whole of creation. You will wonder why they do that, and the answer is that that is how they put themselves in direct contact with the source of life. Yes, for nature responds to their greeting. How often I have gone out into my garden in the morning and greeted the angels of the four elements, the angels of fire, air, water, and earth, and even the gnomes, nymphs, sylphs, and salamanders. And when you do this you can see them dancing and singing for joy. I send greetings to the trees, the rocks, and the wind, too. Try it yourself and you will feel that something inside you slips into place and becomes more harmonious, and that many elements of obscurity or misunderstanding fade from you simply because you have decided to salute living nature and the creatures that dwell in it.

The disciples of a spiritual teaching know that everything is alive; this is why they are attentive to plants, insects, and even stones. Sometimes they will touch a rock gently with their hand, saying, 'Be patient; one day you will be free,' because in every block of stone there is an entity who must remain bound and captive until his prison is shattered and he is set free. Small pieces of rock that break off from the mass enjoy better conditions for their evolution, because little by little they are crushed to powder and mingle with the soil, ready to be assimilated by the vegetable kingdom.

Upon seeing big rocks, disciples can speak to them in other ways, too. They can say, for instance, 'I have such admiration for your patience; when I think that you have been there for centuries, exposed to storms and frost and great heat, and yet you never complain! I congratulate you on your stability and endurance; please let me share some of it.' Perhaps you have the impression that there is nothing very remarkable about this attitude, or even that it is ridiculous. Yet I can assure you that if you do this often, with great faith and trust, something of the strength and stability of that rock will enter you and you will manifest these qualities in your life.

As I say, disciples are extremely attentive to nature and all its invisible inhabitants. For them, the earth is alive and sacred and peopled with innumerable creatures. You might think, 'What difference does it make whether I treat the earth with respect or not? It doesn't feel anything; I'm not doing it either any good or any harm.' Very true, but if I say that you must treat the earth with respect, it is not for the sake of the earth but for your own sake. If you pay attention to stones, plants, and animals, your awareness of the invisible world will develop much more readily. You have probably never thought about that. To be a disciple of an initiatic teaching is to develop the awareness that all the things of nature are alive, and consequently to respect, care for, and protect them; it is to develop a profoundly constructive spirit.

Winning the collaboration of nature spirits

Nature is peopled with innumerable creatures which cannot be seen by man, and they have been given all kinds of different

Le Bonfin

names according to the different countries or places in which they live: elves, fairies, gnomes, salamanders, sylphs, undines, nymphs, dryads, sirens, nereids, naiads, and brownies, etc. And when you are in a forest or anywhere else in the midst of nature, you should be aware that these beings, who are highly developed and very much awake, can see you. It is good to make contact with them, therefore, and show them that you appreciate their work. All these beings are very happy when someone recognizes the beauty and usefulness of their work. When they see that you appreciate what they do, they become your friends and smile and dance for you, and they can even give you certain gifts: vitality, joy, poetic inspiration, or clairvoyance, for example.

And you can talk to them. Go up to a tree, for instance, and tell it how much you admire it: 'How beautiful you are! And how tall and strong and hardy. How marvellous to be able to live for so long... Ah, if only I could have your strength and endurance! Will you please be my spokesman and tell all the other trees in the forest how magnificent you all are and how much I love you? Give them my love!' Then you can kiss the tree goodbye, and it will hand on your message of love to all the other trees. When you do this, hosts of creatures who live in the trees will come out and watch you as you continue your walk through the forest. They show their delight by dancing round you, and you may even see an immense being appearing amongst the trees and looking at you with eyes of light. This is the Lord of the Forest, a sort of egregor or collective soul that combines in himself all the creatures of the forest and who radiates light and colours. When you get home after an experience like that you cannot help but be full of happiness; you sense that this is true life.

You must talk to nature spirits, therefore, and even exhort them to do something for the glory of God: 'Listen to me: what are you doing? You should be helping the Universal White Brotherhood, which exists in order to help human beings and make them wiser, so that the kingdom of God may be established in the world. Lend us your support. Get together and get out all your little trumpets and send the message to the four corners of the earth!' Then all these little beings will respond to your appeal and, like primitive peoples who communicated with tom-toms or smoke signals, they will spread the word and work for the coming of the kingdom of God.

When you are by the sea or sailing on the ocean, you can speak to the inhabitants of the oceans in the same way: 'What are you doing for the kingdom of God? Every time a ship passes this spot you must speak to the human beings on board and tell them to change and improve!' And the water spirits will listen to you and do as you ask. Of course, we know that human beings are not so easily influenced, but that does not matter; at least all those little creatures that you have spoken to are at work already—in fact, they are delighted to be given something important to do. Most of them have no idea what it means to work for a divine ideal; they have no moral conscience. They do not know what good and evil are; they only know that they are afraid of some great cosmic power which is beyond their comprehension. This is why, when an occultist asks them to help him to work black magic, they are perfectly willing to do so. As they have no moral sense, they can be used either for good or for evil, so why not use them for good, for the establishment of the kingdom of God?

Our debt to nature

We are indebted to nature for all that she gives us: air, water, heat, sunshine, etc. And as we cannot pay off this debt with money, we are going to have to pay it in the currency of love, gratitude, and respect, and with our readiness to study everything that is written in her great book. We also pay off some of that debt when we do good to other creatures; when we pass on some warmth and light to them. This is how we pay our debts to nature.

We are under no obligation to pay everything back in the same form: we cannot pay for the air we breathe with air, nor for the water we drink with water. We would not even know how to begin making air or water—not to mention warmth or sunshine. We have received our physical bodies from the earth—there is no getting out of that—and we are going to have to give them back one day. But while we are still alive we are allowed to keep them; nobody is asking us to give them back for the moment. But what we are being asked to give, what we are capable of giving, are our luminous emanations, for human beings were created in the Lord's workshops in such a way that they are capable of radiating and shining and projecting their emanations into the whole universe. They have been given a quintessence of light and the power ceaselessly to amplify and vivify it and send it out into space—on condition, of course, that they practise doing so; otherwise the only thing that will emanate from them will be darkness.

On the physical plane we are strictly limited, but on the spiritual plane our possibilities are unlimited; we can give back a hundredfold all that we have received.

Chapter Nine

The Sun and the Stars

The Sun[1]

Human beings have never really understood how important the sun is. I know that nowadays scientists are taking more and more interest in it, but always for utilitarian purposes: they would be delighted if they could learn to bottle and sell it! It is the material, industrial, and commercial possibilities that interest them; they are a million miles from seeking any spiritual benefit from it. Even religious people—I should say, especially religious people—are quite unaware of this aspect. And it is precisely this spiritual aspect that you must try to understand: what the sun and its rays really are; how to grow spiritually by getting to know the sun and spending time with it; how to look at and contemplate the sun; and how to enter into it and identify with it.

Preparing for the sunrise

If you plan to attend the sunrise, you must prepare yourselves in advance, the day before: be careful not to eat too much or go to bed too late, and avoid doing anything that might trouble

---

1.See Complete Works, vol. 10, which deals at length with the subject of the sun.

or torment you the next morning. In other words, try to do everything in such a way as to be free, with a clear mind and a heart at peace, and with no loose ends to settle, repair, or regret. If you fail to prepare yourselves, your reservoirs wil! be empty when you get up in the morning, and you will be too drowsy to take part in this, the most useful work anyone can do—not only for yourselves but for the whole of humanity, even for the whole universe. For we are part of the cosmos, and we cannot envisage our existence as something apart and separate. If you respect certain rules, therefore, and come up to the Rock[2] in the morning with your mind centred exclusively on this all-important work, knowing that your future, your happiness, your health, and your equilibrium depend on it, you will share in the treasure that flows continually from the divine source, the sun.

Prayer to say while walking up to the Rock

O Angel of Earth, Angel of Water,
Angel of Air, Angel of Fire,
I love you! Be blessed, three times blessed.
And blessed be you, beloved gnomes, nymphs, syiphs,
and salamanders.

Meditation at sunrise

In the peace and light of the morning, you can start your meditation, slowly and gently, without trying to concentrate on the sun too abruptly. Start by glancing inwards to see if all your inhabitants are at peace. If they are making a noise or being rowdy and rebellious, try to calm them down and restore order and balance, for you cannot launch out towards the sun until peace and harmony reign within you.

You must not try to concentrate on the same subject every day, otherwise you will get bored with it. It seems that the mind

---

2.The Rock mentioned here is a natural rocky plateau at the top of a hill near the Bonfin.

is like the stomach: it soon gets bored if you give it the same food day after day. So vary your diet as much as you like, as long as you stick to 'vegetarian' dishes! My role is to give you different methods by presenting new aspects of the sun, so that, each day, when you meditate on the Rock or anywhere else, you can always find one thing that tempts your appetite; the following day you can choose something else.

In order to get the most out of what I say, you should take notes and make yourself a little list, like a cook's list of possible menus, and write down all the methods and formulas I give you and all that I explain about the sun. Then, each day you can look at your list: 'Now, let's see, that doesn't tempt me…nor that. How about this? Yes, that just fits the bill.' Then you will enjoy yourself, because your meditation will be a success. But there is no guarantee that the same method will suit you two days running; so the next day you can change your menu and choose a new subject for meditation.

Themes for meditation

1. Seeking the centre

The sun is the centre of the solar system, and all the planets move harmoniously in orbit round it, and it is this harmonious movement of the planets round the sun that must be duplicated by our own cells. But in order for this to happen, we have to find our own centre: the sun, God, the spirit within us. When we achieve this, every particle of our being moves in rhythm with universal life; and the sensations and states of consciousness that this produces in us are too wonderful to express in words.

The closer we come to the sun in spirit, soul, thought, heart, and will, the closer we come to God, because on the physical plane, the sun is the symbol and the tangible, visible representative of the Deity. All those abstract names by which men designate God—source of life, creator of heaven and earth, prime cause, almighty God, universal soul, cosmic intelligence—can all be summed up in the one familiar, concrete reality of the sun. We can look on the sun as the summary and synthesis of all those sublime, abstract ideas that are beyond our comprehension. On the material plane, the sun is the gateway, the physical link, the medium through which we can be united with the Lord.

When you contemplate the sun in the morning, you are contemplating the centre, the spirit, the eye of God. This is why you must be animated with the desire to draw nearer to the centre, to your own centre. The simple act of looking at the sun brings you closer to the heart of the external solar system as well as to that of your own being: your consciousness draws closer to your own centre, your spirit, from which it draws light, peace, freedom, and strength. The day you decide to work at this in all consciousness, you will sense the movement of the currents and waves flowing between you and the sun, creating forms and colours and a whole new world.

2. Extracting subtle elements from the sun

The sun is the source and father of all things, the prime cause; it is he who engendered the earth and the other planets. This is why the elements contained in the sun can all be found on earth as well, but in a condensed, solidified form. The minerals, metals, precious stones, plants, and gasses, all the dense or subtle bodies found in the ground, water, and air, or on the etheric plane, come from the sun. All the chemical and pharmaceutical products we know here on earth are made from substances that come from the sun. So by focusing all their powers of concentration on the sun, disciples can extract and absorb, in all their original purity, every element they need for their health and equilibrium.

This is extremely simple to do; it is not even necessary to know what elements you need for your health—that is not important. All you need to do is to rise mentally to the finest, subtlest, most rarefied regions and wait there while all these subtle currents wash over you. And your soul and spirit, which are highly skilled chemists who know the exact nature of every etheric substance, will choose those you need and leave aside all the others. Your role is simply to wait in a spirit of love, submission, joy, and trust, and very soon you will feel that something in you has been healed, pacified, and strengthened. That is all you have to do.

It does not matter if, for the time being, you do not know the exact nature of these subtle elements. It is enough to know that they are to be found in the prana. Prana is a living force, the outpouring of vitality from the sun that we breathe in with the air and absorb into every cell of our body. Prana is like a pure stream, cascading down from the mountain heights, its waters charged with every kind of element for the nourishment not only of the fish swimming in its waters but also for the animals and people living along its banks. Prana is a great river flowing from the sun, and by meditation and breathing exercises, we can obtain all the elements we need from it.

3. By looking at the sun we come to resemble it

When you look at an object, you might not realize that it represents either a potential danger or a potential blessing for you. It depends on the nature of the object, its form and radiations, and also on your own inner state, for your whole being takes on the shape, dimensions, and attributes of that object. You will say, 'But human beings don't change shape!' That is true, they do not change shape physically; but inwardly, on the psychic level, a human being identifies with what he looks at: this is a law of nature. When we gaze at the sun, therefore, even if we do not know it, our soul assumes the same shape and becomes a luminous, incandescent sphere. It is the law of imitative magic that is taking effect: we look at the sun and our whole being begins to resemble it.

132 A New Earth

All of you will one day resemble the sun, but only if you gaze at it with great love and trust. In this way you will become warmer and more luminous and better able to vivify others; in the midst of humanity you will radiate light, warmth, and life. If you persevere with this practice for years, consciously reaching out to the sun, the law will manifest itself with great power, and you will become a veritable sun.

4. Bridging the gap between you and your higher self

Imagine that you are already up there in the sun, and that you look down at that creature here on the Rock—this creature that is yourself! You project yourself out of your body and amuse yourself, watching and smiling at yourself sitting down here: 'Oh, look at that funny little creature down there; to think that it's me! How small and puny he looks! But I'm going to help him; I'll give him all the help he needs!' If you do this very simple exercise every day, you will already be starting to rebuild the bridge. Nobody can tell you how long it will take to complete the job, for you are not building with iron, steel, or concrete, but with another, far subtler matter from the mental plane.

Although we do not feel this to be so, part of us—an extremely subtle part that we call our higher self—actually dwells in the sun already. Our higher self is not always present in our physical body; if it were, it would make itself felt with its prodigies. No, it visits us from time to time, manifesting itself to us through a brief contact with the brain; but as our brains are not yet ready to sustain the intensity of its vibrations or to tune in to its wavelength, the contact cannot last long.

This is where our work with the sun comes in: the purpose of our work with the sun, and of all our meditations and prayers, is to restore communication, to build a bridge between our lower self down here and our higher self in the sun. When the bridge has been built and communication restored, we shall once again be united with that higher self that dwells with God in constant happiness, joy, and boundless freedom. Yes, part of ourselves already dwells in God, in a state of indescribable bliss.

You must realize that the sun can help us tremendously in our efforts to bridge the gap between us and our higher self. Without the help of the sun, human beings would probably go on clinging to their philosophy of separateness for thousands of years without ever finding the fulfilment they long for. The time has come to adopt the philosophy of universal unity, which makes us feel our oneness with the Creator and with all the entities of light—angels, archangels, and divinities. With this philosophy, humanity will find its way back to the source far more rapidly and effectively.

5. Visit the sun

Once you have reached the sun, imagine that you go and visit the ruling archangel: picture yourself as you talk to him, as he puts his arms round you and tells you many of his secrets. He will give you some of his light, and from time to time you can send some of what he gives you to that little creature sitting on the Rock, the creature you call 'me', but who is not the real you. Little by little, you will begin to feel your consciousness expanding; heavenly peace will flood into you, and revelation after revelation will unfold in your mind. In this way, you will be developing new faculties of comprehension, and gradually, even though you continue to be just like everybody else outwardly, inwardly you will no longer be the same. You will have become an exceptional being, thanks to the new capabilities that you have developed.

6. Bask in the spiritual sun which makes the seeds in your souls germinate

If the seeds that the Creator has sown in our soul, spirit, heart, mind, and physical body fail to grow and bear fruit, it is because we have forgotten to draw close to the sun. Only the light and warmth of the sun is capable of awakening what the Lord has sown within us: qualities, gifts, and virtues, magic powers and all the splendours of heaven. When human beings understand this and decide to draw nearer to the spiritual sun, all the seeds lying dormant in them will begin to germinate and grow and bear fruit.

Expose yourself to the sun's rays and let them do their work. You will feel a mass of tiny buds and seedlings beginning to grow within you. Of course, you are going to have to water them, otherwise they will wither away. The sun contributes light and warmth, but it cannot water your plants; it needs the co-operation of water, and that is your job, for the water they need is in you. The sun does part of the work, and we have to do the rest; it warms our plants, but it is up to us to water them with our love, faith, trust, and enthusiasm. The sun expects us to lend a helping hand! If you leave it all to the sun, letting it warm you and doing nothing to help, the results will not be up to much, for any shoots that spring up thanks to its warmth will die from lack of moisture.

But how do you actually collaborate in this work? When you are up here in the sunlight, you must be as active as the sun—that is, you must meditate, pray and contemplate, and be grateful to the Lord, or say some good words. In this way you will be watering your seeds with all the love of your heart and setting them on the right path.

7. Finding the Blessed Trinity in the sun

The three persons of the Blessed Trinity—Father, Son, and Holy Spirit—can be found in the life, light, and heat of the sun. The Father is life; the Son is love (or light); and the Holy Spirit is light (or love).[3] Perhaps you will ask, 'But have we got the right to see these infinitely exalted entities as light, heat, and

---

3.See *Complete Works*, vol. 10, chap. 4.

life?' Yes, indeed we have! In fact, the enormous practical advantage of recognizing this correspondence is that it enables us to contemplate and communicate with the Blessed Trinity every morning, and to create bonds through which we can receive its blessings. It is a promise of resurrection and life.

When the world above created the world below, it left its imprint on all things so that man would be able to find his way back to it. Cosmic intelligence, the Trinity, has no desire to remain totally hidden and inaccessible; it manifests itself in the sun so that men may have the possibility of finding it. In reality, the Blessed Trinity is not wholly present in the light, heat, and life of the sun; it is far too great to be contained in the sun. But through that light, heat, and life which pours into our world every day, we can reach out and touch the Trinity: we can talk and communicate with it, love it, and draw it into ourselves. And since each one of us is created in the image of God, we must also be a trinity. Through our mind, heart, and will each one of us is already a trinity that thinks, feels, and acts. Of course, at the moment, this little trinity is cold and numb and does not shine very brightly; but in the company of the sun, it will become warmer, brighter, and more alive. So, once again, we see the point of being present at sunrise: gradually the little trinity that each of us represents becomes as bright, warm, and life-giving as the sun itself; gradually it becomes more and more like the supreme Trinity of Father, Son, and Holy Spirit.

Jesus said, 'Be perfect, just as your Father in heaven is perfect.' But if we have never seen the Father, where can we go to find an example of his perfection? Here, to the sun! Here is the model we need. God is very far above us, very far away, but in his mercy he has given us the means of finding him. He has left signs, a vital lead, and if we follow this lead it will take us all the way through the sun to the Father. The sun points the way.

Every day, we have before our eyes this reflection, this sublime, perfect image of the Holy Trinity, and if we learn how to work with this model, our own little trinity can also become holy. It is all very well to keep repeating Jesus' precept, 'Be perfect, just as your Father in heaven is perfect,' but never having seen the Father, we have no notion of how he manifests himself, of his vibrations and colours, or of his power; it all remains very theoretical. The sun gives us at least a tiny idea of the Godhead, and, above all, it reveals that Father, Son, and Holy Spirit are inseparably one.

According to the Cabbalah, three is one and one is three. In man, too, the three are always united: mind, heart, and will are never separated; they are welded together and advance together as one. The mind makes plans, the heart offers encouragement and support, and the will races to put the plans into effect. Can't you just imagine them running hand in hand! Sometimes, of course, they quarrel among themselves, and then a person gets into trouble because his will has rushed ahead, leaving the intellect behind. The intellect shouts itself hoarse, trying to get the will to wait, to warn it that it is going the wrong way; the will simply answers, 'Shut up, you don't know anything about it!' The three of them have some terrific arguments—but then this trinity is not yet holy! If we want our trinity to be holy, we must take the sun as our model so that its light impregnates our mind, its warmth impregnates our heart, and its life and power impregnate our will.

8. A disciple's rosary

This is an imaginary rosary that you can make for yourself, in which the sun has an important role to play. First of all, choose a moment when you are in a very good frame of mind, and begin by becoming fully conscious of yourself, because you are going to be the first bead on this rosary. Perhaps nobody recognizes you as a bead yet, but that does not matter; you are still rather small, but you will get bigger. The second bead must be your father. You are the centre of your own kingdom but he is the centre of your family, and even if he is none too wonderful at the moment, he is important symbolically; he represents the heavenly Father. Think of him as a symbol and string him on your rosary so that he will be linked to you and to the other beads, for this will help him.

Next, you have to find the chief magistrate of your town, the mayor, and thread him on the string too. He may not be much good as a mayor, but that does not matter either. He is important as a symbol: he is the head of the community; the citizens go to him to express their needs, and when government officials visit your town, it is he who receives them.

Next you have to find a rather bigger bead to represent the head of your country, the head of State, and string him on to your silver thread too. After the head of your country comes the head of the planet, the Regent of the Earth. If you know his name, so much the better, you will be able to thread him on to your rosary all the quicker. He represents a very big bead, for he is far greater and more powerful than the others. Next comes the head of the solar system, the sun itself; immense, luminous, hot, and perfect as he may be, he must be threaded on to your rosary! But you have not finished yet: the last bead on your rosary is the Lord of the whole universe, God himself.

Now you have the seven beads of your rosary, with yourself on one end and the Lord on the other. The next thing to do is to tie the two ends together, so that there is one continuous current flowing from God and passing through the sun, the Regent of the Earth, and so on, all the way to your own father and to yourself, and then from you to God, and so on.

9. An exercise to develop your aura[4]

For disciples, the best protection against negative currents and evil spirits is their aura. The brighter it is, the purer its colours, and the further it extends, the safer they will be, for the

---

4.See also chap. 14.

aura functions as a suit of armour and protects them from harmful currents and unclean spirits.

So you must work to develop your aura when you are watching the sunrise in the morning. See how the sun surrounds itself with an aura of glorious colours and say to yourself: 'I, too, want to wrap myself in the most gorgeous colours: purple, blue, green, yellow, orange, and red.' Then spend a long, long time bathing in that brilliant light; picture its rays reaching out far, far beyond your physical body; picture the blessings it brings to all those who are touched by it, to all those with whom you are in contact in one way or another. In this way your aura will be a protection for you and, at the same time, a blessing for others.

10. Learning to love as the sun loves

Take the sun as your model, for he distributes his gifts of life and warmth to every creature without discrimination, to criminals as well as to holy and upright men. Is the sun blind? Can he not see the crimes that men commit? Or is he only a machine without intelligence or discernment, indifferent to goodness or viciousness, honesty or dishonesty? No, the sun sees the faults and crimes of men better than anyone; but he also sees that these are tiny, insignificant details compared to the immensity of his own warmth and light. All the things that seem to us so monstrous and terrible are little errors to him, just dirty, petty, destructive little incidents. He washes and mends and repairs the damage and continues with boundless patience to help human beings until they reach perfection.

The sun has his own conception of human beings. He knows that the human soul is eternal and immortal, but he knows also that man is still immature, still a hard, sour, unripe fruit. So, as he is very good at ripening the fruit on trees, and knows exactly how to pour sugar and perfume into them to make them juicy and delicious, he wants to help man to ripen too. He recognizes, of course, that man is going to need much longer to ripen than fruit, and he has decided to be very patient. The sun refuses to abandon humanity, because he knows that if he did, their evolution would be stillborn; there would be no more ripe fruit, no more saints, prophets, or divinities on earth. If the sun is still shining, it is because he knows the goal that he is working for and the purpose of creation, and he has decided to go on helping human beings to reach maturity.

The sun is the only being that never gives up. Every other creature gets tired, shuts up shop, and drops out of sight, dead and buried! But the sun is always there, triumphant and radiant. He says, 'Come and slake your thirst, take what you need. Have you done something stupid? I won't hold it against you. Human beings are selfish, vicious, and vindictive, and if they catch you, I can't answer for your safety. But I shall never hurt you; come, drink in my rays... There will always be more for you.'

When you take the sun as your model, you are obliged to become a kinder, better person. You find the courage to forget all the difficulties and disappointments caused by your fellow human beings. When you begin to think like the sun you become a divinity, for you are never at a loss for love or patience. Everyone else may end by giving up and turning you out: 'Go away. I don't want to see you any more! I've done all I can for you and now I'm tired.' But the sun is never tired. You can see now why I want to lead you to the sun: because he, and he alone, can fill you with noble, divine sentiments.

11. Let your love go out to all mankind

When disciples are too involved in their own personal problems, they are not free to be open and have broader interests; they are too busy thinking of themselves. But as soon as they begin to see their way more clearly and solve their own problems, as soon as they are a little freer, they can begin to concern themselves with the whole of mankind and become like the sun. In fact, even if a disciple has the care of twenty, fifty, or a hundred people, it is never enough; he is so free that he feels the need to extend the scope of his love and concern to the whole human race. He pictures humanity as a single person, and a constant stream of love and many-coloured rays of light pours from the superabundance in his heart. When people are still preoccupied with themselves, their family, and friends, they are not capable of such happiness. But disciples who have learned to pour out their love and light on the whole of humanity—without worrying about the number or whereabouts of the individuals involved—resemble the sun.

12. Go to the sun for the solution to all your problems

When you have a problem or a difficulty, talk to the sun about it as though you were talking to a person: 'My dear Sun, what would you do in my place?' The sun will smile (children always draw the sun with a broad smile on his face) and say, 'If I were in your place I would have committed suicide long ago! Wouldn't it be much better to put yourself in my place? Why should I climb down into your place? It's not possible. It is you who have to climb up and put yourself in my place. And if you were in my place you would do thus and thus.' He will give you the advice you need—the very same advice that I am giving you!

13. Formulas to say at sunrise

Here are some formulas that you can repeat as you are watching the sunrise. Wait until the first rays become visible, and then say, silently:

As the sun rises over the world, so may the sun of truth, freedom, immortality, and eternity rise in my spirit.
As the sun rises above the world, so may the sun of love and immensity rise in my soul.
As the sun rises above the world, so may the sun of intelligence, light, and wisdom rise in my intellect.

As the sun rises above the world, so may the sun of gentleness, kindness, joy, happiness, and purity rise in my heart.

As this luminous, radiant sun rises over the world, so may the sun of strength, power, force, dynamic energy, and activity rise in my will.

And as this luminous, radiant, living sun rises over the world, so may the sun of health, vitality, and vigour rise in my body.

Amen. So be it, for the kingdom of God and his righteousness.

Amen. So be it, for the glory of God.

14. Rise above the clouds

When you sense that certain negative thoughts are beginning to cloud your 'sky', weaken your faith and love, and dull your perception of the splendour of God or the beauty of the teaching, then it is time to concentrate and project rays of the utmost purity in the direction of these mists, and it will not be long before you see things becoming cleaner, purer, and brighter. It is by means of thought that one rises above the clouds. Thought is like a rocket or a beam of light. You can aim or focus it on a given point: the source of life, the eternal sun, your inner centre, or the Lord himself, and within a few minutes it will pierce the clouds, however thick they may be, and you will find yourself up above, bathed in crystal-clear light.

15. The colours of the spectrum

When you look at the light of the sun through a prism, you discover a world of untold richness and splendour. It is written in the Book of Zohar: 'Seven lights are there in the most high, and therein dwells the Ancient of Ancients, the Secret of all Secrets, the Hidden of all Hidden Ones: Ain Soph.'

There are seven lights: red, orange, yellow, green, blue, indigo, and purple.

The spirit of red light is called the spirit of life. Red is associated with life and with the love of all creatures.

Orange is the spirit of sanctity. Orange light improves one's health and gives one the desire for perfection.

Yellow is the spirit of wisdom. It incites us to read, reflect, meditate, and seek wisdom, and to be guided by reason and prudence in our actions.

Green is the spirit of eternity and of evolution. It is associated with growth and development, and also with wealth. If we associate green with hope it is because it helps human beings to advance on the path of evolution.

Blue is the spirit of truth. This colour is also associated with religion, peace, and music. Blue develops a sense of music. It pacifies the nervous system, heals the lungs, and is beneficial to the eyes, which are the symbol of truth.

Indigo is the spirit of strength, the spirit of royalty. It has approximately the same properties as blue.

Purple is an extremely subtle, mystical colour which leads human beings to the higher regions. It is the spirit of divine omnipotence and spiritual love; it is the spirit of sacrifice. Purple is a very powerful colour which protects people, facilitates astral projection, and helps them to understand the love of God and other worlds.

In order to advance your evolution you can meditate every day on the colours and on the virtues and qualities they represent. Work with a different colour every day. You can begin with red, the colour nearest to the earth, for instance, and progress from red to orange, yellow, and so on, up the scale. Or you can start with purple and work downwards, whichever you prefer.

16. Spiritual grafting

There is a science that you must learn in order not only to remedy your faults and passions and inferior tendencies but to use them and take advantage of them: this is the science of grafting. Men first discovered and developed the technique of grafting in order to improve the quality of fruit, but when it comes to the psychic or spiritual domain they are not nearly so capable or ingenious. Perhaps you are wondering where you can get hold of the cuttings you need. I will tell you. There is one major distributor, one who is infinitely more intelligent, more loving, more powerful, and more generous than anyone you could ever find on earth, and he has a storehouse full of cuttings which are ideal for the grafts you need. That being is the sun.

So speak to him and ask him for the grafts you need. Tell him: 'O beloved Sun, I am too stupid; I don't seem to understand anything! When I want to express my ideas they are so confused that I can only stutter and stammer, and I am always getting into trouble. But you who are so luminous, you who give light to the whole world, graft some of your intelligence on to me.' And he will. He will give you cuttings free of charge, and you can graft them into your brain. In fact, he will even send you an expert to help you if you are not sure how to do it. Later, you can ask him for a cutting of love or health or anything else you need; he has them all. But do not ask for everything at once; it is better to have these cuttings one at a time, otherwise some of them will wilt and die from lack of attention.

17. Exercise for days when clouds hide the sun

There will always be days when the sun is hidden by clouds, and you should know what to do when that happens. On days like that, when conditions are not conducive to conscious mental activity, you must shift the centre of activity to the level of the subconscious, to the solar plexus.[5] Abandon yourself to the cosmic ocean of love and bliss. Entrust yourself in utter confidence to God, saying, 'Lord God, let me be borne away on the ocean of light; I put all my trust in you.' And, keeping just a tiny flame alight within you so that nothing bad can slip in, you let yourself drift away on an ocean of joy and beatitude. This is how you can work on a cloudy day: just let yourself be cradled in peace, thinking of nothing—but without falling asleep, of course—and simply glancing into yourself from time to time to see what is going on.

18. Look at the sun with new eyes every day

Every day I think to myself: 'Yesterday, I thought I knew the sun, and now, today, I realize that I had not really understood; but today I'm beginning to understand.' And the following day I find myself thinking the same thing. Whereas you say 'Oh, I know all that. That's old stuff!' When you begin to think that, when you think that you have nothing more to learn, that you know it all, that is when you begin to stagnate and go to sleep, and all progress comes to a halt. You must never do that. Every day, be sure to say to yourself: 'Ah, today I'm beginning to see what the sun really is; I'm just beginning to understand.' If that is your attitude you will continually make progress. This is just another new and wonderful method.

19. The elixir of everlasting life

The elixir of everlasting life is an exceptionally pure liquid that is capable of unblocking all the channels and ducts of our physical bodies, and it exists in profusion throughout nature. Those who possess it have simply managed to condense it. It is present in the earth and in plants, in the oceans and rivers, in mountains and in the air we breathe, and, in a very special way,

---

5.See chap. 12.

in the sun's rays. But it is present in such highly diluted, homoeopathic proportions, that all kinds of special instruments would be needed to collect and condense it and store it up. When we attend the sunrise in the morning, this is what we are looking for: this elixir which flows through nature like a stream of living water. Every atom of prana, every minute globule in suspension in the air, is filled with a spiritual essence. When our whole being is concentrating on the sun, our bodies absorb these minute particles which purify, strengthen, and vivify us.

20. Drawing down heavenly fire

Just as physical fire has the power to make iron sufficiently pliant and tractable to be given a new form, so the heavenly fire of divine love has the power to plunge man into a spiritual state in which he sloughs off his warped, crooked form and receives a new, bright, harmonious one.

The first thing to understand, therefore, is that in order to change all your old ideas and habits and transform your character, and even your heredity, you must call on heavenly fire. You must beg it to come into you, to envelop and inflame your heart and your whole being. Do not rely on explanations from other people or from books: they can do nothing for you if you are not alight with the blazing fire that makes you as alive as the sun. For the sun is living fire, and it is by going to see the sun rise every morning that we renew our contact with this fire from heaven. If you forge a close bond with the sun, if, whole-heartedly and with all the powers of your intelligence, you let the sun set you on fire, flames will begin to rise from you and enfold you in their burning heat.

The Holy Spirit is none other than the sacred fire of the sun.

21. Drink the sun

Suppose you are sitting up there on the Rock waiting for the sun to rise and expecting the first ray to appear over the horizon at any moment. You are wide awake and attentive, and as soon as that first ray of sunlight appears, you suck it in as though you were drinking it. Instead of just looking at it and breathing it in, you eat and drink this living light and picture it flowing into all the cells and organs of your body, strengthening, vivifying, and purifying them.

This exercise can be tremendously useful by helping you to concentrate, and the results can be fantastic: your whole being starts to quiver, and you begin to feel that you are really and truly drinking light. Try it—drink the sun. The exercise will help you to remain wide awake and conscious: the need to keep drinking will keep you alert.

22. The philosophy of unity

You must work at making everything within you converge towards a single goal. You must tame and harness all your disparate, contradictory tendencies and convince them to pull together as one; you must impose your will on them and make them your slaves. And when you have welded all these energies into one, when you are capable of launching them as a single unit towards one glorious, luminous, beneficial goal, you will be a focal point of such intense, powerful light, that, like the sun, you will be able to radiate light in all directions.

Take this idea and meditate on it at sunrise: how to unify your inner forces; how to free yourself from all that contradicts, hinders, or opposes your ideal; and how to amplify all that stimulates you and spurs you irresistibly forward. In this way, night and day, new energies will flow from you and converge in the direction of your divine goal.

The Stars

Night shows up the relativity of things

Daylight shows up the importance of the things of earth, whereas night shows us how unimportant and petty they really are. If you have problems, cares, and worries, if someone has wounded your feelings or done you an injury, contemplate the stars in the night sky and you will feel all these little irritations fading into nothingness. You will feel that you are above them, that you become nobler and more generous; you will even laugh at injuries and insults. In the face of this immensity, in the face of the solemnity and majesty of the universe, how can you continue to dwell on such petty little problems? How can you keep moaning and groaning for all the world to hear? I have known astronomers who admitted that their work had completely changed their way of looking at things: all the little inconveniences and struggles of life took up far less room in their lives, and they were constantly amazed by all the fuss people made about little things.

The language of the stars

You must also learn to work with night and the stars. What sweetness! What a marvellous climate of peace and tranquillity the night affords—exactly the conditions one needs to melt into the vastness of space. Lie on your back in the grass on a summer night, when everybody else is asleep and the stillness of the night is broken only by the chirping of crickets and the occasional croaking of a frog, and gaze up at the multitude of stars in the immense sky. Try to understand them, to penetrate the secret of these worlds and the entities and intelligent beings who inhabit them. Stay there a long time, and pick out a star which seems to attract you more than others, with which you feel a greater affinity; love it, make friends with it, imagine that you go and talk to it or that it comes down to talk to you.

Several times, when I was very young, I climbed to the top of Mount Musala[6] and spent the night there. I did not understand everything that the stars told me, but I loved them; my soul was filled with the wonder of them. They glittered and shone and winked at me, and I gazed at them for such a long time with such love that I, too, began to wink and blink, and finally fell asleep. The next morning I would go down to the camp to wash before going to watch the sun rising. Night and day... in this way I linked them together in one work. And now I am beginning to realize that although I did not understand everything that the stars whispered to me, my soul heard and recorded it all, and it has kept those records intact. It is only with time that one gradually understands the revelations of the stars.

What do the stars talk about? They tell the sublime story of the glory of the eternal Lord.

6.Mount Musala in the Rhodope Mountains is the highest peak in Bulgaria (3,000 metres).

Chapter Ten

Mental Work

Thought enables man to extract the quintessence

Most human beings live their lives on such a superficial level that they have become incapable of envisaging anything else. They have never considered working with the untold possibilities of the mind, and yet no other type of activity can equal mental work.

Let me illustrate this with some simple examples: when you extract copper or iron ore from a mine, it takes many tons of ore to produce even a small quantity of pure metal. All the rest is the gangue, or rock, which is worthless. In the same way, to obtain a few litres of Bulgarian essence of roses, you need several wagon-loads of rose petals, but the essence you extract from it is so rare that it is worth a fortune.

Most human activity consists, as it were, in displacing masses of soil and rock, the crudest forms of matter, whereas the work of the mind makes it possible to extract the essence from the mass. If you never learn to use your minds to concentrate and to control and master yourselves, to direct your energies and use them for a higher purpose, the results of your activity will be like wagon-loads of ore. They will simply be a burden to you unless you can extract the essence.

The work of an initiate is to extract from matter its quintessence, without which everything is insipid and meaningless. Even if you possess all the wealth in the world, if you do not possess the quintessence that exists on the mental plane, you will always feel a void; you will always feel deprived, dissatisfied, and restless. It is not quantity that gives meaning to life, but quality, quintessence.

Thought must only be used for good

Generally speaking, people who are concerned with the things of the spirit know that thought is a force that can acquire shape and form and give birth to concrete realizations, but they do not realize how deeply a thought can disrupt the great cosmic body of which we are all members. They never stop to ask themselves whether the plans they pursue so relentlessly fit in with God's plans, and they strain and struggle with unbelievable violence to get what they want. They must understand that thought must not be used to demand money, seduce women (or men), or obtain any of the things that life seems to be refusing them. Thought must be used only and always for the good of others; it must have an impersonal, altruistic aim: the happiness of all humanity and the triumph of the kingdom of God on earth.

The role of music in the work of the mind

Music represents a very powerful current, and it is capable of giving us tremendous impetus. This is why we should use it to strengthen our fidelity to our ideal and to recapture the precious spiritual moments we have known in the past. We should listen to music in order to bring out the best in us; music must be a wind that fills the sails of our ship and drives us onward, towards our heavenly predestination.

Concentration, meditation, contemplation and identification

If you try to force yourself to concentrate when you are in a state of agitation, you will be doing violence to your cells. You have to be diplomatic with your cells; do not let them suspect that you are going to demand an effort of them. Begin by calming them and then, gradually, tactfully, and gently, steer them towards your objective. In this way you will be able to concentrate on whatever you choose. You must proceed step by step until you reach such perfect and powerful balance that all your cells are swept along in the movement and give you their full co-operation. In this way you can orientate your thought so clearly and so well that it will continue to advance in the same direction every day.

Meditation is an activity of the mind which seeks to fathom spiritual truths.

Contemplation is an activity of the heart or soul which lingers enraptured before the beauty and light of an image, quality, or virtue and enters into communion with it.

And over and above meditation and contemplation is identification, the magic work of the will, of the spirit, which identifies with the Creator in order to create.

Meditation

Meditation is like mastication: when you chew a mouthful of food, the salivary glands start to function and you absorb the subtler, more spiritual energies contained in the food through your tongue. When you meditate it is as though you were 'chewing' a thought. But, of course, it is meditation only if the thoughts you are chewing are of a philosophical, spiritual, or mystical nature. The role of meditation is to lead you to a higher world and bring you light and peace.

1. Meditation as a means of realization

It is best to begin by meditating on subjects that are readily accessible. Human beings are so designed that abstractions do not come naturally to them. They need to begin by grasping something tangible and visible, something familiar and attrac-. tive. Suppose that you are attracted by beauty, for instance, or intelligence, and that you decide that you would like to have it. Try to concentrate your imagination on yourself as you would like to be; contemplate that ideal self that you want to become, and you will feel an influx of joy, confidence, and vitality, as though you were already tasting a future reality. Do this exercise: for a period of ten or twenty minutes, imagine that what you long for has already been achieved; see yourself standing close to God, bathed in divine light and accomplishing magnificent deeds. If you use thought to prepare the way, it will lead you closer and closer to the fulfilment of your wishes.

However, be sure to examine your wishes and plans very carefully, for if they are too personal, if they are not in harmony with the order that God has established throughout creation, they will conflict with the divine laws, and with other lives and entities and a whole vibratory order of being that already exists, and they will not succeed. Or, if they do succeed, you will be even worse off than before. In these circumstances it would be better to fail; then at least you will be spared many disappointments and mishaps, and, since you have not succeeded in doing the wrong you wanted to do, you will not be punished for it.

2. The two most excellent subjects for meditation

a) To be an instrument in the hands of God

You can meditate on all kinds of things: health, beauty, wealth, intelligence, power, or glory, and all these subjects are good. But the best exercise is to meditate on God himself, in order to be steeped in his love, light, and strength, in order to live for a brief moment in his eternity. Always meditate in order to serve God, to do his will and be one with him. If you do this you will feel yourself to be a totally compliant instrument in his hands, and God himself will think, feel, and act through you. In this way you will be abandoning yourself to the omniscient will of wisdom and light which will guide you in all your ways.

b) To bring heaven down to earth

Since human beings have been sent to live on earth, the must try to find out why. What are they here for? Jesus said, 'Thy will be done on earth as it is in heaven.' 'On earth as in heaven' means that heaven must be brought down to earth. And the 'earth' is our own personal earth, the earth of our physical body. This means that once we have worked to reach the summit, heaven, we must come down again and organize things on earth. Immortality is on high; light and harmony are on high. And is there any reason why everything that is on high should not be made incarnate here below in the physical world?

Christ's philosophy is to bring heaven down to earth, to establish the kingdom of God and his righteousness on earth. This is the kingdom that Jesus was working for, and he asked his disciples to work for it also. So this is where we have to work, here on earth, beginning with our own physical bodies.

So there you have the two best subjects for meditation: how to devote yourselves entirely to the service of the Godhead, and how to go about bringing heaven down to earth as a concrete, physical reality. The whole meaning of life is contained in these two activities. Other activities have their significance, of course, but nothing else has the divine significance of these two activities.

Contemplation

Contemplation is an activity of the soul. The whole of one's being participates in this act in which the soul pours itself out, immolates itself and becomes one with the object of its contemplation.

Contemplation is the highest form of prayer. Prayer is the stepping-stone by which you rise to the contemplation of divine splendour, and in the face of that splendour your heart expands with joy and you are borne up into a state of ecstasy in which your consciousness expands a hundredfold and you feel that you are embracing the whole universe, that you are becoming as all-encompassing as the Lord himself. All those who have experienced the raptures of contemplation have had the sensation of being no longer on earth in their physical body; they felt as though they were being submerged and melting into one with the universal soul. Later, of course, they were obliged to return to earth and take up their daily tasks, but for a few minutes or a few hours, they dwelt in infinity, in fusion, and in ecstasy.

Identification

The goal of all spiritual work is identification with the Deity. In India, the initiates expressed this in the phrase: 'I am he,' meaning that God alone exists and I am nothing more than a reflection, a repetition, a shadow of God. No creature has a separate existence; we are all part of the Lord. He is the only being that is, and we are simply a projection of him. When disciples say, 'I am he,' they are saying that they have no existence apart from God, and that by consciously strengthening the bond that unites them with the Lord, they will resemble him more and more, until one day they too will be creators.

Prayer

1. The best of all prayers

As we do not know what plans God has in mind for us, we must ask him to enlighten us, and if there are still some dark

THE SYNOPTIC TABLE

PRINCIPLE	IDEAL	NOURISHMENT	PRICE	ACTIVITY
SPIRIT	ETERNITY	FREEDOM	TRUTH	IDENTIFICATION
SOUL	THE INFINITE	IMPERSONALITY	ECSTASY	PRAYER ADORATION CONTEMPLATION
INTELLECT	KNOWLEDGE LEARNING LIGHT	THOUGHT	WISDOM	MEDITATION
HEART	HAPPINESS WARMTH	FEELINGS	LOVE	HARMONIOUS & ARTISTIC ACTIVITIES
WILL	POWER MOVEMENT	STRENGTH	GESTURES BREATH	BREATHING GYMNASTICS
PHYSICAL BODY	HEALTH	FOOD	MONEY	PHYSICAL WORK

This table, given by the Master Omraam Michaël Aïvanhov, shows how the spiritual life is nurtured and sustained on the level of the different subtle principles that constitute man's psychic being, just as his physical life is sustained on the level of his physical body.

areas that we do not understand, we must implore him to take possession of us. We can say: 'Lord, I still do not understand, but please do what needs to be done. Make me do your will even without my knowing it. Use me, seize hold of me, take possession of me, come and dwell within me.'

It sometimes happens that we cannot see what God wants us to do at a given moment. Of course, we know the overall orientation: goodness, disinterestedness, sacrifice, love and abnegation, kindness and generosity, and so on. But there are times when we cannot tell exactly what he wants of us. So, since we are lacking in clairvoyance and lucidity, we should ask that the Lord's will be done, in spite of us if need be. It is not given to all men to have a very clear perception of the usefulness or value of what they want to do. Sometimes we do God's will without knowing it.

This is why we must implore and clamour (with threats, if necessary) to be used by heaven. Say, 'At last I understand. I know that I can do nothing about my lower nature; it is too stubborn, tough, and corrupt. It will never change. I beseech you, O heavenly entities, send me the most marvellous, perfect creatures to act in its stead, to guide and instruct me and take control of my life. I shall never be able to change this lower self, even in hundreds and thousands of years, so bind it hand and foot and replace it with luminous spirits capable of making it obey them, so that in spite of myself I may carry out your plans.'

When you say, 'Lord God, enter into me and take the place of my personality; take the control of my life into your own hands,' you are doing something that has an effect not only on the material particles of your physical body, but especially on the memory and on the ingrained patterns of your cells, and old habits are replaced by new faculties, qualities, and virtues. This is one of the very best prayers you can possibly say. All other prayers contain a personal element, an element of self-interest; they are designed to curry favour with the Lord. Whereas with this prayer you lay your life before him and say, 'Yes, Lord, I am willing to die and disappear. Take my life but, I beg you, send heavenly entities to take the place of my lower nature so that I may serve you.'

2. A method to help you to pray

You often complain that you pray but that you get no results, so let me give you a very simple and very effective way of making contact with the Lord. When you want to pray, begin by creating a picture in your mind of a vast multitude of spirits scattered in every corner of the world, each one of which is focused on the Lord. If you unite with these beings and join your prayers to theirs, you will no longer be a lonely voice crying in the wilderness of life: you will be one with thousands of other beings of light who are also calling on heaven. This kind of prayer is always heard because of its collective voice; and at the same time, you will also benefit from it.

It is because you act alone that your prayer fails to achieve its goal. The secret of success is to unite yourself with all those who are praying, for at every moment there are beings at prayer somewhere in the world.

Thought possesses all powers

True disciples are convinced that thought is a reality and that it is endowed with every possible power. Knowing this, even when they find themselves in circumstances that cause suffering and bitterness to themselves or to others, disciples can continue to act on the level of thought. They do not have to waste time bemoaning their fate, and no one can prevent them from working: they are free, beyond the reach of adversity, true creators.

Those who are not accustomed to working with thought are always complaining that they do not have what they need, that they are persecuted and hampered. They have a thousand reasons to be miserable, because they have not yet discovered that God has given human beings all the powers they need, but on the plane of thought. The day they learn to take advantage of every circumstance in life and, by the power of thought, use it in order to rise to a higher level, they too will be beyond the reach of adversity.

Chapter Eleven

Spiritual Galvanoplasty

What is galvanoplasty?

Galvanoplasty is the process used in electro-plating, in which two electrodes are introduced into a solution of metallic salts: usually gold, silver, or copper. The anode, or positive pole, is a sheet of the same metal as that in the solution, and the cathode, or negative pole, is a gutta-percha mould coated with graphite and stamped with the design of a medal or coin. The two electrodes are also connected to the two poles of a battery, and when the current is switched on, a film of metal is deposited on the cathode. At the same time, the metal of the anode is decomposed, thus providing a constant supply of the precious

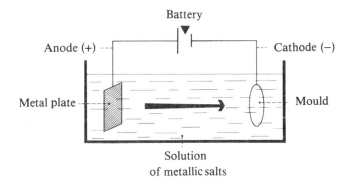

Battery

Anode (+) ---

Cathode (−)

Metal plate ---

Mould

Solution
of metallic salts

metal in the solution. Little by little, the cathode is completely coated with the metal from the solution, and you have what you intended: a medal of gold, silver, or copper bearing a design. (See figure, p. 163).

The phenomena involved in galvanoplasty are reflected in different areas of life, in particular in the work that goes on in a mother's womb during the period of gestation, as well as in the spiritual life.

A mother's work during gestation

Metaphorically speaking, a pregnant woman has within her all the elements used in galvanoplasty: the electrodes, the mould, and the solution. The mould, which is the cathode, is the living seed implanted in her womb by the father, and it bears his image: the image of a drunkard, a criminal, a perfectly unexcep-tional being, or that of a genius or saint. As soon as a woman is pregnant, a current of energy flows from her brain to the seed, for the brain is connected to a battery (the stars, God), from which it receives these currents before transmitting them to the embryo. The mother's blood represents the solution in which the anode and cathode (the brain and the uterus) are immersed—for our blood bathes all our organs and cells—and it contains all the necessary metallic salts: gold, silver, copper, and so on.

The anode (the mother's mind) constantly renews the supply of precious metals (her thoughts) in the blood. The seed provided by the father may be of very exceptional quality, but if her thoughts are of lead (symbolically speaking), she need not be surprised if, later on, her child is born enveloped in lead—that is to say, if he is unhappy, frail, and often ill.

But if a mother knows the methods used in gold-plating, she can decide to apply them in bringing her child into the world. As soon as the seed (the cathode) is implanted in her womb, she places a sheet of gold in her mind (the anode), the gold of a sublime ideal and of the loftiest thoughts. The current is switched on, and the blood flowing through her body conveys the precious metal to the seed. The child grows, clothed in gold, and when it is born it will be robust and healthy, beautiful in body and mind, and capable of overcoming disease and all the difficulties and evil influences it may encounter.

Most mothers believe that it makes no difference what they think about during pregnancy, that their thoughts cannot influence the child in their womb. They think that it will be time enough, once it is born, to start taking care of it and looking for teachers and educators. No, when a child is born it is already too late: no teacher or educator on earth can transform a child if the material used to form it in its mother's womb was inferior in quality; it will always be pretty much what it was. If it is as dull as lead, however much you slice bits off it to make it shine like silver, it will tarnish again immediately; by which I mean that the child will always fall back into its innate defects, however good an education it gets.

You must understand how important it is for a pregnant woman to fill her mind with elevated, luminous thoughts. Thanks to her thoughts, the seed that is growing within her absorbs these pure, precious materials, and instead of giving birth to a child that is stupid, ill, or criminally inclined, she will bring into the world an artist, a scientist, or a saint, a messenger from God.

When a woman is ignorant of the laws of galvanoplasty she may entertain all kinds of inferior thoughts and satisfy all the most outrageous fancies and cravings that come to her at this time. She does not realize that she is being duped by the harmful entities that swarm round every pregnant woman. These entities hope to have some part in the life of her child later on, so they try to upset the process of galvanoplasty. They know that if it is badly done they will be free to go in and out of the child's soul at will, to feed on it and use it for their own ends. And the same is true of the beautiful entities of light that the mother succeeds in attracting.

Galvanoplasty in the spiritual life

The phenomenon of galvanoplasty also teaches us how to nurture the purest and most noble thoughts and feelings in our minds and hearts in order to develop to the full all the qualities our heavenly Father placed in us when he created the world. When we have brought these qualities to their full flowering, our visage will be that of our Father: the visage of perfect love, wisdom, and truth.

We must work every day, therefore, according to the rules of galvanoplasty: firstly, by filling our minds with thoughts that represent materials that cannot tarnish, thoughts of pure gold; secondly, by carrying constantly in our heart and soul the image of a truly exceptional being (Jesus or another great master); thirdly, by 'plugging in' to the central powerhouse of life-giving forces. In this way we immerse ourselves in the solution of cosmic ether, whose forces work in us and accomplish their wonders. Day after day, subtle particles of matter flow from our spirit into every cell of our body, and under their influence, our faces and even our bodies change, until one day we become a true likeness of God.

A person who always has the picture of a particular being before their eyes begins to resemble that person or thing, thanks to the phenomenon of galvanoplasty. Two people who love each other and live together, or who constantly think of each other, end by looking alike. In fact, I am sure that you have often seen the resemblance between a man and his dog: sometimes it is the dog that begins to look like his master, and sometimes, unfortunately, it is the man who begins to look like his dog!

So there are certain laws which we can learn to use in order to further our evolution, and if you have understood me correctly today, you will begin to do so without delay. Enshrine the image of a being who is truly beautiful, strong, pure, wise, and full of love in your spirit, and contemplate it with adoration; little by little you will begin to look like the object of your contemplation.

You are probably thinking that it is difficult to achieve the transformation of oneself by looking at a picture. That is true: it cannot be done in a day or even a week. But if you persevere with patience and faith, you will eventually see results. The first step is to understand that you are constantly being dragged downwards by all kinds of horrifying images which you are still carrying about within you, and that you must replace those images of the past with that of a master—Jesus, or another great initiate—and let this new image become your true love. For love is the primordial force which accomplishes the greatest transformations.

Chapter Twelve

The Solar Plexus

The importance of the solar plexus[1]

The solar plexus governs many of the functions of our physical body; breathing, elimination, nutrition, growth, the nervous system, and the circulation of the blood are all influenced by the solar plexus. At the same time, the solar plexus is in contact with the entire cosmos and serves as the medium through which man communicates with the universe. As you can see, it is an extremely important organ, and we must avoid whatever makes it tense, for this leads to the contraction of the blood vessels and other ducts in the body, and the blood and other fluids cannot flow freely. When this happens, waste products are deposited on the walls of the vessels, and this leads eventually to serious health problems.

How to strengthen one's solar plexus

The disorders that most disturb the solar plexus and, consequently, the abdominal organs (liver, kidneys, stomach) are fear, anger, worry, doubt, licentiousness, and chaotic thoughts and feelings. The solar plexus is our reservoir of life-forces, and

---

1.See *Complete Works,* vol. 2, for further explanations concerning the solar plexus.

it is completely demagnetized and drained of all its reserves by such disorders.

But if the solar plexus can be emptied, it can also be refilled, and it is this that disciples have to learn: how to replenish their solar plexus.

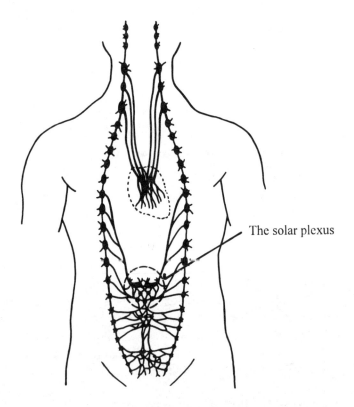

The solar plexus

Let me describe some methods you can use:

1. A tree is a reservoir of forces that come both from the sun and from the earth, and it is possible for us to draw on those forces. Choose a big, strong tree—an oak, beech, or pine, for instance. Stand with your back against it, with your left hand

between the tree and your back, the palm pressing on the tree trunk; at the same time, place the open palm of your right hand on your solar plexus. Concentrate mentally on the tree and ask it to give you some of its strength. When you do this, you receive a transfusion of energy through your left hand which passes through your right hand to your solar plexus. When you have finished, remember to thank the tree.

2. You can also strengthen your solar plexus by watching and listening to running water—a fountain, a spring, or a waterfall, for instance. This method may seem insignificant, but it is very effective, for the running water influences the solar plexus, which begins to get rid of harmful waste matter.

3. When you meditate on very elevated, divine subjects, place your right hand on your solar plexus to fill it with strength and energies that you can draw on later. You can use this method whenever you feel full of joy and strength: instead of wasting these treasures in useless gestures, words, thoughts, and feelings, place your hand on your plexus and meditate for an instant as you fill it with that strength and joy. Our solar plexus is a bank in which we can deposit our savings so that they are there later when we need them. This is something you can experience every day for yourselves.

The brain and the solar plexus

The solar plexus is a brain in reverse: in the brain the grey matter is on the outside and the white matter on the inside; whereas in the solar plexus the grey matter is on the inside and the white matter on the outside. It is the solar plexus that created the brain and continues to nourish it and send it energy and strength. When the energy from the solar plexus fails to reach the brain, you become lethargic and incapable of activity; you have a headache or feel sleepy and incapable of thinking clearly. The brain, therefore, is not totally separate from the solar plexus, but there are not very many human beings who know how to direct energy from the solar plexus to the brain.

The brain is dynamic and active, but it tires very quickly if its efforts are not sustained by energy from the solar plexus. This is why, before undertaking any major intellectual task, before meditating or concentrating, you should prepare your solar plexus. One way to do this is to massage it in a circular motion, anticlockwise. In a very few minutes you will feel that your thought is flowing freely and you can begin work. Your activity must be harmoniously and evenly shared between the brain and the solar plexus.

The feet and the solar plexus

It is more than likely that in your everyday lives you have already noticed a connection between the feet and the solar plexus. When your feet are very cold, for instance, there is a certain tenseness in your solar plexus, and if you eat at that moment, you will have trouble digesting your food. Whereas, if you soak your feet in hot water, you have the agreeable sensation of feeling your solar plexus relaxing, and that puts you in a good mood.

So, when you feel demagnetized, troubled or tense, prepare a basin of hot water and soak your feet in it, washing them with conscious attention. In this way you will be influencing and reinforcing your solar plexus, and you will immediately feel much better. And if you are trying to meditate at home one day and find yourself incapable of doing so, have a foot bath, and you will soon be able to concentrate much more easily.

Chapter Thirteen

The Hara Centre[1]

1.For a fuller treatment of the hara centre see *Complete Works*, vol. 6, also *Man's Subtle Bodies and Centres*, vol. 219 in the Izvor Collection.

The hara centre is situated four centimetres below the navel. According to Japanese sages, the hara or navel chakra is man's life-centre, his centre of gravity, the universal centre; and when a person concentrates on it and develops it to the full, they become tireless and invincible. The most striking thing about those who have worked to develop their hara centre is that they are exceptionally well balanced.

Exercise to develop the hara centre

Sometimes, when they are meditating, initiates fold their hands over their belly. They do this when concentrating on the region of the hara centre in order to stimulate the circulation of energies for the nourishment of the rest of their body. And you can do the same: for a few minutes every day, place both hands on your hara chakra and concentrate on sending it a great deal of love. Do this exercise in whatever position you like—lying down, sitting, or standing—but be careful not to arouse the energies dormant on the level below. This exercise is designed to stimulate certain spiritual energies that will give you a sensation of stability, strength, and liberation.

The hara centre or chakra is mentioned in many esoteric books, but often in very different ways. For instance, in his book,

The Twelve Keys, the famous alchemist Basil Valentine urges adepts to descend into the centre of the earth in search of the philosophers' stone. In fact, of course, Valentine was not talking about descending into the centre of the planet Earth, but into our own centre, into our own physical bodies, for it is there that we can find materials, treasures, and wealth of every sort.

The Indian sacred scriptures tell us that Brahma resides in the belly, Vishnu in the region of the heart and lungs, and Shiva in the brain. Why should Brahma, the creator, be said to dwell in the belly? Well, when you look at the human body you see that this is where life is created. Yes, life springs from this centre. Even in the Gospels it says, 'From his belly will flow rivers of living water.' Why the belly? Why not the brain or the lungs? What is so special about this region of the body, that living waters should flow from it? Yes, Brahma, the Father, the creator, dwells in this centre, but it takes years and years of work before you can feel his presence and communicate with him.

And a very profound meaning lies behind the account of Jesus' birth in a manger. The manger in which Jesus was born is the hara centre, the navel chakra, and each time a human being comes to birth in the spiritual world, it is this same event that is happening all over again. This is what initiatic science calls 'the second birth'. The birth of Jesus in a manger is an initiatic symbol of the deepest significance. It is here, in the hara chakra, in this crib flanked by the ox and the ass—the liver and the spleen—that a disciple has to bring to birth the divine infant, the new consciousness, the child Jesus.

Chapter Fourteen

Methods for Working with Light

Light must be your constant preoccupation

You must continually seek the light and concentrate on it. Eat and drink light! Attach more importance to light than to any other treasure on earth. As soon as you have a free moment, close your eyes and fix your mind on the image of the light that pervades all things: the source of all blessings.

While you are waiting for a train, or for an appointment with the dentist, instead of reading the rubbish you find in magazines, spend a few minutes thinking of light.

When you are out on the street, stop in front of a shop window for a few moments as though you were looking at the goods on display, and concentrate for a few seconds while you light your inner lamps. When you go on your way again you will feel refreshed and cleansed.

This exercise can be used in all circumstances: if you are cooking, writing letters, washing, dressing, or undressing, you can always take a few seconds to picture in your mind the light that bathes the whole universe. Many clairvoyants have actually seen it; they have seen that all creatures, all objects, down to the very stones of the earth, are not only bathed in light, they emanate light.

When we are meditating together in silence, put all your cares to one side and concentrate on light as though everything, even your very life, depended on it. Imagine that you are living your last moments, that you are about to leave the world and that you must cling to light, for it is the only thing that can save you. Light! Nothing else matters.

Picture it white and brilliantly incandescent, and join your voice to that of the initiates, who declare, 'I am a particle of particles of the incandescent soul.' You can also conjure up a vision of purple, blue, green, yellow, orange, or red light; but it is preferable to work with white light, for white light combines the qualities of all the other colours in one. White light contains the omnipotence of purple, the peace and truth of blue, the wealth and eternal youth of green, the wisdom and knowledge of yellow, the health, vigour, and vitality of orange, the activity and dynamic energy of red. But it is white light that is primordial.

When you are capable of being totally focused on light, when you begin to sense it as a vibrant, throbbing, quivering ocean of peace, happiness, and joy, then you will also begin to perceive it as perfume and as music—the cosmic music which we call the music of the spheres, the song of the universe.

There is no more worthy, more glorious, or more potent work than this work with light. If you really want to devote yourself to something truly great and noble, this is it; there is none other.

The light that pacifies and heals

When your soul is overshadowed by grief, difficulty, or doubt, go and talk to the light about it. Say, 'O Light, you who are the most intelligent of all beings, enter into me and bring light to my heart and mind.' And the light will come to you and make everything bright and clear.

If you want to help those who are in difficulty, send them rays of light, imagine that they are being penetrated through and through by those rays.

And if you are in pain, call on light to come and heal you; imagine rays of light of different colours streaming from your fingers to the painful spot, and before long you will feel the pain easing.

The elixir of everlasting life is condensed light.

The light that protects

If you want to protect yourself against someone who uses violence and tries to impose certain limits on you, wrap yourself—and your aggressor—in light, and they will be unable to carry out their evil designs.

If you have to be out alone at night and are afraid of being attacked, call on the light to walk beside you, and it will come and keep you company and protect you. (Obviously, you must be sensible and not expose yourself to danger unnecessarily or thoughtlessly in the belief that heaven has nothing better to do than to watch over you whatever you do!) It is not the criminals themselves who sense the presence of light; it is the evil spirits that accompany them who are terrified by it and urge them to keep away from you.

The light that brings harmony and love

If you want your family to live in harmony, picture your house bathed in light.If you want your friends to be pleased to see you when you go to visit them, concentrate for a few moments before you go into their house, and send some light in ahead of you. Most people go and see their friends when they are depressed, irritable, or worried and want to be cheered up. This is a sure way to lose their friendship!

If you want to win people's love, you must realize that the only way is to use light. All other means—money, seduction, or violence—are forbidden. The only means acceptable to heaven (and also the only truly effective means) are to send them gifts of spiritual light, to surround them with light. If you want someone to think of you and love you, therefore, send them light, and when their soul receives these beneficial waves, it will appreciate you more and more and begin to take an interest in you.

Send out signals of light

The world is like a vast ocean in the dark of night, and you are like so many little boats drifting rudderless on that ocean. If you want luminous spirits from on high to come and rescue you, you have to light your lanterns and send up flares to let them know where you are. In other words, you have to radiate light so that the sublime spirits can find you in the midst of darkness. The Gospels tell us to pray, and to pray is to send light waves up to heaven. The entities of the invisible world will have nothing to do with a light that has been snuffed out, so if you want to attract their attention you must light your lanterns.

A collective exercise with light

Concentrate and imagine that you are all enveloped in a brilliant sheath of light that radiates with such splendour that our gathering forms an immense sun, a sun capable of lighting up the whole world. Each one of you should feel like a luminous sun, pulsing and shimmering with light and sending out rays that join and mingle with the light from all the others to form a single gigantic sun.

Then introduce this sun into your heart and mind and contemplate the multi-coloured rays flowing from it. While you are doing this exercise, forget everything else and, all together, concentrate on radiating light for the whole world.

Light, the image of God

Imagine a dazzling light in which everything—suns, angels, and archangels—throb and vibrate as though they were fused into one infinite ocean. This ocean of light into which all forms melt and blend is the true image of God.

Chapter Fifteen

The Aura[1]

1.For a fuller treatment of this subject, see *Complete Works*, vol. 6.

All living creatures—human beings, animals, plants, and even stones—emit particles and produce emanations, and it is these particles and emanations that we call the aura. The aura of a human being is the combined emanations of all his or her different bodies: physical, etheric, astral, mental, causal, buddhic, and atmic; and the emanations of each one of these bodies contribute their own particular shade of colour. The aura, therefore, is a vast synthesis of a person's different tendencies, qualities, and virtues. Some people's auras are immense, reaching far beyond their physical bodies, with intense vibrations and splendid colours. Others, on the contrary, form only a thin layer of dull, dingy light round their physical bodies.

The aura is a protective shield

An aura that is in good condition is the best possible protection anyone can have. All the upheavals in the world are powerless to harm you if your aura is pure, luminous, and strong, for it is a shield against harmful currents and disturbances of every kind. Disciples who are surrounded by an aura like that are, as it were, in a fortress; when others all round them are uneasy, distressed, or exhausted, they are still full of courage and

love, because they feel themselves to be inhabited by an inner
light, and thanks to that inner light, they can also help others.

The colours of the aura: a frame of reference

If you want to be capable of distinguishing truth from
falsehood in every circumstance, you need a frame of reference,
a yardstick by which to recognize truth, and you can possess this
yardstick only if your aura has a lot of blue in it. The true shade
of blue will be your guide.

If you want wisdom and intelligence, you can obtain them
thanks to the yellow in your aura, and so on.

How to develop your aura

You can work in two different ways to develop your aura.

The first method is to use your conscious will to imagine that
you are immersed in the purest and most luminous colours. If
you use this method you will need a prism, for the only way to
have an accurate idea of the seven colours, is to decompose the
white light of the sun through a prism. The colours that you see
in nature—in flowers, birds, and crystals—are only an
approximation of the true colours. You can only obtain a true
red, yellow, green, blue, purple, and so on, by using a prism.

You can vary this method by imagining that all the colours
radiate from you out into space. Picture yourself at the centre of
a sphere, sending out rays of love, in the form of colour and
light, to the whole universe.

The second method consists in cultivating the virtues: purity,
forbearance, generosity, kindness, hope, faith, humility, justice,
and disinterestedness. This second method is the most effective,
for if you concentrate all your energies on developing the virtues
they will take care of your aura: your love will make it more
vivid, your wisdom will make it more luminous, your strength of
character will make it stronger, and the purity of your life will

make it more limpid and transparent. The qualities that manifest themselves in your aura depend on the virtues you develop.

Of course, the best of all is to combine the two methods, for if you concentrate on the colours of your aura every day while continuing to live a very ordinary life and making no effort to cultivate the virtues, you will be building something up with one hand and tearing it down with the other. This is why it is better to do both: live a pure, honest life, full of love, and at the same time work consciously to develop your aura. As your aura gains in breadth and beauty it will enable you to be in communion with every region in space.

Chapter Sixteen

The Body of Glory[1]

1.See also *Complete Works*, vol. 5, chap. 11.

The New Testament tells us that we possess an incorruptible body of pure light, which we call the body of glory. In the very distant past, this body enabled human beings to travel through space and to see and understand the whole of creation. But as they became more and more deeply immersed in the denser layers of matter, humans neglected their body of glory until it became incapable of manifesting itself; and now we have to reverse this movement and nourish and care for it so that it can be restored to its former function. It is thanks to our body of glory, after all, that we shall live eternally and recapture the powers that were ours in the past: one day, the animals will obey us and the spirits serve us once again. All the forces of creation are at the disposal of those who nourish their body of glory until it attains its full stature, for it is in this glorious body, not in our physical body, that God dwells.

How to develop your body of glory

What do you do with a seed? You plant it, and then you take care of it and keep it watered, and it sprouts and grows and becomes a tree, that is to say, a strong, full-grown body. The body—or tree—with all its beauty and all the fruit it will bear when it reaches its full stature is potentially present in the seed, but we have to nourish and water it, otherwise it will die.

Our body of glory is there, within us, in the form of a seed, a germ, and the task of a disciple is precisely to water, warm, and nourish this seed. When you experience some moments of intense spiritual life, or listen to music, or are deeply moved by the sight of something very beautiful, you are nourishing and reinforcing your body of glory. These feelings of love and wonder, these emotions, are the particles with which you nourish this body within you, just as a woman nourishes the child in her womb with her thoughts and feelings as well as with her blood.

You can only nourish your body of glory with the purest and most luminous elements; this is why you must be very careful to filter out all impurities of thought and feeling. And if you experience a difficult moment and are besieged by feelings of hatred, jealousy, or revenge, remember that this can retard the formation of your body of glory, and immediately change your state of mind.

Our body of glory can only be formed by the best in us, and if we nourish it for a long time with our own flesh and blood, our own fluid, our own life, it will become bright and radiant, strong, powerful, and immortal, because it will be formed of eternal materials that cannot corrode or tarnish. It will accomplish marvels, not only within us but also all round us.

You will ask, 'But how can we get hold of the materials we need?' and the answer is: by means of the law of affinity. Each of your thoughts, feelings, and desires draws from the surrounding atmosphere matter which exactly corresponds to it. Good thoughts, feelings, and desires, backed up by a firm intention, capture particles of pure, eternal, incorruptible matter. If you work every day to acquire this matter, it will enter and pervade your whole being and drive out any mouldy, worn-out, dusty particles it finds, until your physical, etheric, astral, and mental bodies are completely regenerated.

Also, every particle of matter is linked to a corresponding force, and the purer the matter the higher its rate of vibration, and the greater its capacity to attract forces corresponding to its purity. Therefore, when you replace the worn-out particles of your body with new, pure particles found in the celestial regions above, you are also attracting to yourself kindred currents and forces. In this way, every time you rise to the divine world and contemplate it in the form of light, beauty, music, and harmony, you gather new particles which, as they are all alive, never come alone; they bring with them their corresponding forces, energies, and spirits.

So you must surpass and transcend yourselves, in order to draw the purest and most luminous particles from the etheric ocean and weld them into your body of glory. You are already capable of obtaining these particles today; in tiny quantities to begin with, but gradually, day by day, in greater and greater quantities. That is what you are doing every day at sunrise: you leave the earth and link up with heaven, with the sun; and the sun gives you some bright, shining particles to add to your body of glory.

Chapter Seventeen

Formulas and Prayers

Formula for motorists

Lord, protect us from ourselves
and those around us.
Keep us safely in your light,
Send us an angel to guide us.

*

Formula to staunch bleeding

By the blood of Adam came death;
By the blood of Christ came life;
Blood, cease your flow!

(Repeat 3 times)

*

Formulas given by the Master Peter Deunov

Niama lubov kato bojiata lubov,
Samo bojiata lubov é lubov.

There is no love like the love of God;
Only the love of God is love.

Niama mãdrost kato bojiata mãdrost,
Samo bojiata mãdrost é mãdrost.

There is no wisdom like the wisdom of God;
Only the wisdom of God is wisdom.

Niama istina kato bojiata istina,
Samo bojiata istina é istina.

There is no truth like the truth of God;
Only the truth of God is truth.

Niama pravda kato bojiata pravda,
Samo bojiata pravda é pravda.

There is no justice like the justice of God;
Only the justice of God is justice.

Niama dobrodétel kato Christovata dobrodétel,
Samo Christovata dobrodétel é dobrodétel.

There is no virtue like the virtue of Christ;
Only the virtue of Christ is virtue.

Niama slava kato Christovata slava,
Samo Christovata slava é slava.

There is no glory like the glory of Christ;
Only the glory of Christ is glory.

Niama sila kato silata na douha,
Samo silata na douha é sila bojia. ˙

There is no strength like the strength of the spirit;
Only the strength of the spirit is strength of God.

*

Formula of consecration

Burn some incense and say:

By the boundless omnipotence of the sacred name of God, Yod, He, Vau, He, and by the omnipotence of the divine Mother and of the magic Word, may all impure and malicious entities be banished from this place (or object).

I consecrate this place (or object) to you, O Lord God, our Father, O divine Mother, O Christ, O Holy Spirit, for your honour and glory, and for light, and may hostile forces never take possession of it.

*

Prayer for harmony

Begin by establishing harmony between yourself and God, the creative principle and first cause. Say:

My God, I have always been foolish and ignorant, but now I recognize my faults and am ready to do better: please forgive me. From now on I want to live in harmony with you. Give me your light that I may no longer break your laws. Allow me to contemplate you. I promise to obey you and do your will.

Next, you turn to the angels and archangels:

Holy angels, so often, when you have brought messages from the Creator to warn or enlighten me, I was deafened by the tumult of my passions and unable to hear your voice. I beseech you to continue to send me light, for I want to obey you. I know that you are the Lord's most exalted servants: I respect and love you.

Then you can speak to the masters and benefactors of mankind, to all those who have made the supreme sacrifice for the divine cause:

O masters of humanity, I have never listened to you because I valued human knowledge above all else. But now I know that what you have discovered and understood is the only essential truth, and I want to help and serve you. Send me some of your learning and knowledge.

Then you establish harmony between yourself and your fellow human beings:

Beloved brothers and sisters, may peace and harmony reign in our midst. Let us forget each other's faults and failings; let us forget the evil we may have done to each other, and work side by side in the Lord's vineyard so as to transform the earth into a garden of paradise in which we may all live as brothers and sisters.

Speak also to the animals:

When God first created the world you lived in peace and harmony with man; it is by our fault that you have become cruel and have to survive under such difficult conditions. I send you light to help you advance rapidly on the path of evolution.

Speak to plants:

O lovely plants, flowers, and trees, you who are willing to stay still and submit to all weathers; what a wonderful example you give us. Thank you for nourishing us; thank you for the beauty and fragrance of your flowers. I send you thoughts of love; I want to live in harmony with you. Give me your freshness and purity in return for my love.

Speak to the stones of the earth:
O you who bear the weight of humanity, you who give us the ground under our feet and the inspiring example of your age-old stability, you who give us materials for our houses and all kinds of beautiful buildings, give us also your strength, and we in turn will give you ours, so that one day you may awaken to consciousness. May there be harmony henceforth between us.

Close your eyes and say to the whole universe:
I love you, I love you, I love you. I am in harmony with you.

*

Prayer for our guide

Lord God almighty,
creator of heaven and earth,
master of the universe,
source of everlasting life,
bright light of the world,
love and plenitude:
With our whole heart, our whole soul, and our whole spirit, we beseech you to grant our prayer: send your spirit of love, wisdom, and truth to abide in our guide and teacher so that he may carry out your plans for the establishment of your kingdom and your righteousness on earth and the coming of the golden age among mankind.
And may we all participate fully in this glorious task of proclaiming you throughout the world as love, beauty, and splendour.

Amen. So be it.

Prayers for different occasions

Lord, do not give me so much
that I forget you,
or so little,
that I rebel against you.

*

Lord my God, do what you will with me; use me
for the glory and success of your kingdom.
All that I have belongs to you,
I promise to do your will.
My God, I am your servant.

*

Lord God, give light to my mind. May I see all things just as
you created them. Light up my path.

*

Lord, grant that I may disappear in your eternity and your
immensity; take my place and dwell within me. Manifest
yourself:
through my intelligence as wisdom,
through my heart as love,
through my will as power,
So that the kingdom of God and his righteousness may be
established on earth.

*

A heart as pure as crystal,
A mind as luminous as the sun,
A soul as vast as the universe,
A spirit as powerful as God and one with God.

*

Lord, I love your wisdom,
I believe in your love,
I hope in your power.
(Repeat 3 times)

*

Appendix

EXPLANATION AND DESCRIPTION
OF PHYSICAL EXERCISES

Excerpt from a talk given on July 19, 1979

What quantities of methods I have already explained to you in my talks! I have given you exercises, gestures, and formulas that you can apply in every circumstance in life to transform negative states, pacify and harmonize yourselves, and help you to link up with heavenly entities. It is sad to see how most people who do not know these methods live, think, and act mechanically, unconsciously. That is why nothing they do produces any significant results: their words and gestures are ineffectual because there is no clear thought or specific purpose behind them.

Today I want to emphasize this point by throwing new light on the gymnastics that we do together every morning. Each exercise is very easy to do and the whole series takes only a few minutes. In fact, at first sight, they may seem rather futile. But they are not designed to be repeated for hours on end in order to develop your muscles. No, there are far more important things to develop than muscle, for even physical strength is not exclusively a question of muscle; you must certainly have seen evidence of this in yourself.

212 A New Earth

There are days when you can walk and run, pick up heavy loads and transport them from one place to another, and you wonder where you find the energy to do all that. And then there are other days when the slightest gesture costs an effort, and you have to drag yourself through the day. What has happened to you? It is simply that the energy—the electric current, the impulse—has ceased to flow from your brain to your muscles, so your muscles remain flabby. And where is that energy supposed to come from? From your nervous system. That is why you must learn to protect and strengthen it.

And this is precisely what we are doing with these gymnastic exercises, for they reach certain centres in our nervous system and nourish, strengthen, and harmonize them, so that we become capable of carrying out the most formidable tasks.

There is an extremely important rule known to initiatic science, according to which each of our activities must reach all three worlds: the physical world, the world of feeling, and the world of thought. You have been doing these gymnastics for years now, and if you have achieved almost nothing, it is because you do not know how to work on the level of the three worlds. If you did, you would obtain powerful results that would benefit not only you but the whole Brotherhood, and even the whole world. Once again, therefore, I shall show you how the word—whether it is pronounced out loud or not—becomes effective when it accompanies a gesture, a feeling, a thought, an intention, a movement of the will.[1]

First exercise. Raising your arms over your head and running your hands down your body, all the way to your feet, say: *'May all the blessings of heaven pour down on me and on the Brotherhood for the glory of our heavenly Father.'*

You must not ask for heaven's blessings for yourself alone; you must help the whole Brotherhood by calling down heavenly

---

1.For a detailed explanation of the exercises see the descriptions and illustrations in the following section.

blessings on it, too. Why do everything only for your own benefit? It is so petty! Why are you always too economical and miserly to say even a few words to benefit others? It is because you do not know how to work with divine forces that you struggle perpetually against the same difficulties. You must mobilize all the powers and possibilities that God has given you—word, thought, and gesture—and put them to work for the good of the whole world.

Second exercise. As you bring your hands up from your feet, along the length of your body to the top of your head, say: *'May all my cells be magnetized, vivified, and resuscitated for the glory of our heavenly Father.'* All the cells of your body will be activated and rejuvenated.

Third exercise. Swing your arms alternately in a forward movement as though you were swimming, saying: *'May I learn to swim in the ocean of cosmic light for the glory of our heavenly Father.'* Yes, always for the glory of God, for no other reason. Your intention will be noted on high by those who are watching you, and they will say, 'Ah! There's someone who is truly working for the Lord!'

Fourth exercise. Swing your arms together from side to side as though you were scything, and say: *'May all my ties with the evil one be severed and broken for the glory of our heavenly Father.'* Human beings never realize that invisible bonds bind them to the powers of hell. They cannot see them, so they continue to eat, drink, and amuse themselves, and practise their shady deals, and all the time they are tied up, bound hand and foot, and dragging their chains behind them. They think they are free; in fact, they think they are pretty wonderful! You must sever these bonds and free yourselves for the glory of God; always for the glory of God.

Fifth exercise. While you are balancing on one foot, say: '*May perfect balance reign throughout my being for the glory of our heavenly Father.*' And if you think of anything else while doing this exercise you will fall over! The only way to keep your balance is to concentrate on one thing, one thought, and let nothing else interfere and distract you.

The organ of equilibrium is in the ear, and the ears represent wisdom. We have to be wise and reasonable in order to keep our balance; when we do not live wisely, when we break the law, we always knock something off balance.

Sixth exercise. Kneel on one knee and bring both hands up to your face and then thrust them out in front of you, saying: '*May all the enemies of the Universal White Brotherhood be put to flight, banished, rejected...for the glory of our heavenly Father.*' The enemies of the Universal White Brotherhood are not men and women; they are the spirits of darkness that enter men and women and use them in order to manifest themselves and destroy God's work. This is why we have every right to drive them out; for some we even have the right to say, '*May they be ground to dust, struck down, and annihilated.*' Do we not have the right to say this? Do they have the right to obstruct the work of light unchallenged?

Seventh exercise. As you thrust both arms out in front of you and then bend backwards, say: '*May all my cells and organs be supple for the glory of our heavenly Father.*' Try to bend back as far as possible without falling over.

Finally, the **eighth exercise** is similar to the first, and you repeat the same formula: '*May all the blessings of heaven pour down on me and on the Brotherhood for the glory of our heavenly Father.*'

These exercises will help to strengthen your will, so that eventually, thanks to your strength of will, nothing will be able to stand up against you; you will triumph over all your difficulties. If you do no exercises you will never have a strong will. Other people can give you knowledge or wealth; others can spark emotions in you; but nobody else can give you will-power. You have to develop that for yourself. This is why the very first thing that initiation requires of disciples is that they should develop and reinforce their will through exercises and discipline. This is difficult, of course, but it is the most effective way, because if your will is strong you can work and persevere, and in the end you will get everything you want: intelligence, beauty, health, power. Whereas, if you are weak-willed, you will get nothing more than you already have; in fact, you are liable to lose what you already have.

Description of the Exercises

General remarks:

– The exercises should be done slowly and rhythmically, with a supple, flowing movement. With the exception of the eighth, each exercise is done six times.
– The starting position is the same for each exercise: standing upright with feet joined and arms hanging straight down.
– The formula corresponding to the exercise should be repeated mentally with each movement.

FIRST EXERCISE

'May all the blessings of heaven pour down on me and on the Brotherhood for the glory of our heavenly Father.'

1. Raise your arms slowly on either side of you, palms up, until the tips of your fingers touch over your head.

2. Just before your fingertips touch, step back with the right foot. Slide your hands down each side of your head...

3. and down the left side of your body.

4. Bend your legs very slightly and lean forward from the waist...

5. as your hands slide down to the ground.

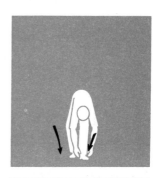

6. Straighten up slowly...

7. bringing your arms up vertically above your head.

8. Just before your fingertips touch, step back with the left foot and slide your hands down each side of your head...

9. and down the right side of your body.

.10. Bend your legs very slightly and lean forward from the waist as you slide your hands down to the ground.

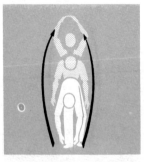

11. Straighten up slowly, bringing your arms up above your head.

12. Just before your fingertips touch, step back with the right foot and, once again, slide your hands down each side of your head and down the left side of your body.

13. Bend your legs and lean forward from the waist as you slide your hands down to the ground.

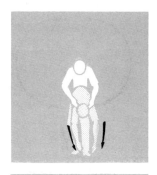

14. Straighten up slowly, bringing your arms above your head. Just before your fingertips touch, step forward with the right foot and continue the movement as before.
Repeat the whole movement, once more, bringing the left foot forward, and once again, bringing the right foot forward.

15. At the end of the last movement, your arms are above your head. Bring your left foot forward beside your right foot, and lower your arms on either side of your body, palms turned down.

SECOND EXERCISE
'May all my cells be magnetized, vivified, and resuscitated for the glory of our heavenly Father.'

1. Raise your arms on either side of you, palms upwards, until they are in a vertical position above your head,

2. As your hands come together over your head, step back with the right foot, turn the palms of your hands forwards, and move your arms slightly apart.

3. Bend forward, bringing your hands down to the level of your left ankle,

4. Straighten up slowly, sliding your hands up...

5. along your left leg...

6. and up the left side of your body.

7. When your hands are on the level of your chest, turn them upwards from the wrist, palms turned towards each other, and slide them up on each side of your face...

8. until they join over your head, the fingertips touching the top of your head.

9. Raise your arms to a vertical position while turning your palms forward and drawing back the left foot.

10. Bend forward, bringing your hands down to the level of the right ankle...

11. slide your hands up...

12. along your right leg...

13. and the right side of your body. On the level of your chest, turn your hands up again, palms turned towards each other, and bring them up on each side of your face...

14. until they join over your head, fingertips touching the top of your head. Raise your arms again and, when they are fully stretched up, step back with the right foot.

15. Bend forward, bringing your hands down to the level of the left ankle.

16. Slide your hands up...

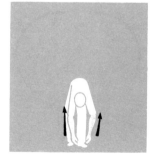

17. along your left leg...

18. and the left side of your body. When they are level with your chest, turn your hands up again, palms turned towards each other, and bring them up on each side of your face...

19. until they join over your head, fingertips touching the top of your head. Raise your arms again and, when they are fully stretched up, continue the movement by stepping forward with your right foot, then with your left foot, finally with your right foot.

20. At the end of the sixth movement, bring your left foot level with the right, and lower your arms on either side of your body, palms turned down.

THIRD EXERCISE
'May I learn to swim in the ocean of cosmic light for the glory of our heavenly Father.'

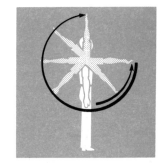

1. Raise your right arm horizontally in front of you, then bring it, in a circular movement, down, back, and up.

2. When your arm reaches a vertical position, step back with your left foot, then slowly bend forward from the waist, bringing your right hand forward and down to your right foot.

3. Stand upright again.

4. Repeat the first movement with the left arm.

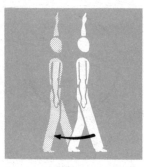

5. When your left arm is vertical, step back with the right foot.

6. Bend down from the waist, bringing your hand down to the left foot.

7. Stand upright again.

8. Raise your right arm horizontally in front of you, then bring it in a circular movement, down, back and up.

9. When your arm reaches a vertical position, step back with your left foot...

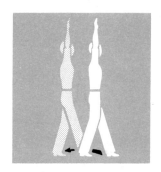

10. then slowly bend down from the waist, bringing your right hand down to your right foot.

11. Stand upright and continue the exercise, moving forward:
   – swing the left arm and step forward with the left foot,
   – swing the right arm and step forward with the right foot,
   – swing the left arm and step forward with the left foot.

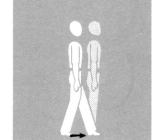

12. At the end of the exercise, bring your right foot level with the left.

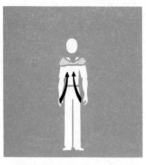

FOURTH EXERCISE
'May all my ties with the evil one be severed and broken for the glory of our heavenly Father.'

1. Raise your arms in front of you to shoulder level, palms turned down.

2. Swing both arms to the right until the right arm is in line with the shoulder, and the left arm is folded horizontally in front of your chest.

3. Step back with the right foot.
1st movement: lower both arms slightly before bringing them back to shoulder level.

4. *2nd movement*: bend slightly from the knees and the waist as you swing your arms from right to left...

5. and straighten up again... ·

6. until you are back in position 2, but with the left arm stretched sideways and the right arm bent in front of your chest.

7. Step back with the left foot.
1st movement: lower both arms slightly before bringing them back to shoulder level.

8. *2nd movement*: swing your arms from left to right as you bend slightly from the knees and the waist...

9. and straighten up again...

10. until you are back in position 2, with the right arm stretched sideways and the left arm bent in front of your chest. Step back with the right foot.

11. *1st movement*: lower both arms and then bring them back to shoulder level.

12. *2nd movement*: bend slightly from the knees and the waist as you swing your arms from right to left...

13. and straighten up again...

14. until you are back in the position with the left arm stretched sideways and the right arm bent in front of your chest.
Continue the exercise by:
– stepping forward with the right foot,
– stepping forward with the left foot,
– stepping forward with the right foot.

15. At the end of the sixth movement, bring your left foot level with your right foot and, simultaneously, bring your arms out in front of you, parallel to each other, palms downwards.

16. Stretch your arms out on each side of you, still at shoulder level, and then bring them down beside your body.

FIFTH EXERCISE

'May perfect balance reign throughout my being for the glory of our heavenly Father.'

1. Raise your arms on either side of you to shoulder level, palms up, then bend your arms and...

2. bring your fingertips to rest on your shoulders.

3. Bend your right leg, bringing the foot up to touch the back of the left knee.

4. Swing your right leg out sideways.

5. Bend the right leg again, bringing the foot up behind the left knee.

6. Swing the right leg out sideways again.

7. Bring the right foot up behind the left knee for the third time, then...

8. step back with the right foot.

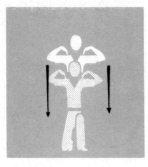

9. Genuflect on the right knee.

10. Stand up.

11. Bend your left leg, bringing the foot up to touch the back of the right knee.

12. Swing your left leg out sideways.

13. Bend the left knee again, bringing the foot up behind the right knee.
Repeat movements 12 and 13 once more.

14. After bending your left leg for the third time, step back with the left foot.

15. Genuflect on the left knee, and stand up.

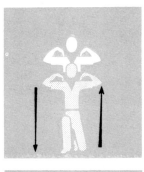

16. Bend your right leg, bringing the foot up to touch the back of the left knee.

17. Swing your right leg out sideways.

18. Bend the right leg again, bringing the foot up behind the left knee.
Repeat movements 17 and 18 once more.

19, After bending your right leg for the third time, step back with the right foot.

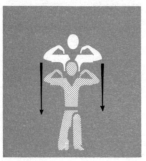

20. Genuflect on your right knee.

21. Stand up.

22. Bring your right foot up in front of your left knee, then...

23. swing it out to the right.

24. Bring the right leg back again with the foot in front of the left knee.

25-26. Repeat movements 23 and 24 once.

27. After bringing the right foot up in front of the left knee for the third time, step forward on to it...

28. and genuflect on to the left knee.

29. Stand up and repeat movements 22 to 26
   - once while balancing on the right leg and swinging the left leg;
   - once while balancing on the left leg and swinging the right leg.

30. After the final genuflection, stand up and bring the left foot level with the right, stretch out your arms at 45 degrees to each side, palms turned towards each other, then, turning your palms down, lower your arms.

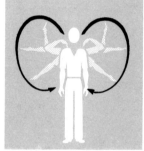

SIXTH EXERCISE

'May all the enemies of the Universal White Brotherhood be put to flight, banished, rejected... for the glory of our heavenly Father.'

1. Stretch your arms sideways and up, palms up...

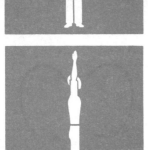

2. then turned towards each other.

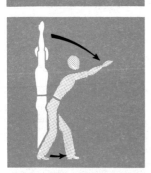

3. Step forward with the left foot and, simultaneously, lower your arms to shoulder level in front of you.

4. Kneel down on the right knee.

1. In order to make this exercise easier to understand, some of the figures show a side view and some a view from above.

5. Bring your hands up to your face...

6. and then slide them down to the level of the solar plexus.

7. Bring your hands up again. When they are on a level with your chest, close your fists and continue the upward movement of the hands.

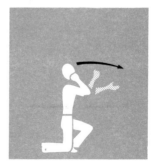

8. When your fists are at shoulder level, throw your arms forward with a vigorous movement, simultaneously breathing out sharply. When your arms are fully extended, open your hands.
Repeat movements 5 to 8 five times.

9. At the end of the sixth movement you are still on one knee, with your arms outstretched in front of you.

10. Bring your hands to your face, palms turned towards you, simultaneously breathing in,

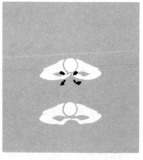

11. then turn your palms outwards,

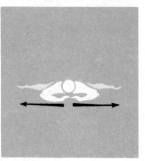

12. and throw your arms out to each side, while simultaneously breathing out sharply.

13. Turn your palms towards the front and bring your fully extended arms forward until they are parallel to each other in front of you.
Repeat movements 10 to 12 five times.

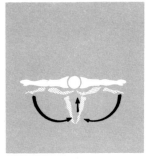

14. At the end of the sixth movement, stand up, keeping your arms stretched out on either side, palms turned towards the ground.

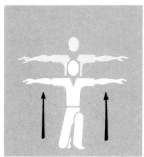

15. When you are fully upright, slowly lower your arms.

SEVENTH EXERCISE
'May all my cells and organs be supple for the glory of our heavenly Father.'

1. Move the left foot slightly forward.

2. Keeping your weight on your left leg, bend the left knee and lean forward and downwards, while simultaneously taking a long step backwards with the right leg.

3. Raise your arms so that they extend forward and slightly upwards, in line with your body, then bring your right foot slightly forward until it is just behind the left while, simultaneously, returning to an upright position.

4. Transfer your weight to your right leg as you start to bend your trunk backwards.

5. Bend your right knee slightly as you stretch your trunk backwards (bending back as far as possible) and let your arms hang down freely on either side.

6. Straighten up...

7. and return to position 2.
Repeat movements 2 to 6 five times.

8. At the end of the sixth movement, bring your right foot level with your left foot and your arms straight down on either side.

EIGHTH EXERCISE
'May all the blessings of heaven pour down on me and on the Brotherhood for the glory of our heavenly Father.'

1. Raise your arms sideways until they are in a vertical position, palms turned towards each other over your head.

2. Then bring your hands slowly down on each side of your head...

3. and down your trunk.

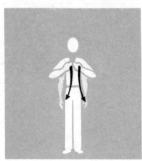

4. Let your arms hang down on either side of you.

Do this exercise three times in all.

By the same author :

'Complete Works' Collection

VOLUME 1 – THE SECOND BIRTH

1. The Second Birth – 2. 'Ask, and it Shall be Given to You. Seek, and You Shall Find. Knock, and it Shall be Opened to You.' – 3. Truth is Hidden in the Eyes – 4. Wisdom is Hidden in the Ears – 5. Love is Hidden in the Mouth – 6. Love, Wisdom and Truth – 7. The Master of the Universal White Brotherhood - Peter Deunov – 8. The Living Chain of the Universal White Brotherhood.

VOLUME 2 – SPIRITUAL ALCHEMY

1. Gentleness and Humility – 2. 'Except Ye Die Ye Shall Not Live' – 3. Living in Conscious Reciprocity with Nature – 4. The Unjust Steward – 5. Lay Up for Yourselves Treasures – 6. The Miracle of the Loaves and Fishes – 7. The Feet and the Solar Plexus – 8. The Parable of the Tares – 9. Spiritual Alchemy – 10. Spiritual Galvanoplasty – 11. The Mother's Role During Gestation.

VOLUME 5 – LIFE FORCE

1. Life – 2. Character and Temperament – 3. Good and Evil – 4. Pitting Oneself Against the Dragon – 5. Presence and Absence – 6. Thoughts are Living Entities – 7. Unwanted Guests – 8. The Strength of the Spirit – 9. Sacrifice – 10. A High Ideal – 11. Peace.

VOLUME 6 – HARMONY

I. Harmony – 2. Medical Science Must be Based on Initiatic Science – 3. The Future of Medicine – 4. A Disciple Must Develop His Spiritual Senses – 5. What Can We Learn From a House ? – 6. How Thought is Materialized on the Physical Plane – 7. Meditation – 8. The Human Intellect and Cosmic Intelligence – 9. The Solar Plexus and the Brain – 10. The Hara Centre – 11. The Initiatic Heart – 12. The Aura.

VOLUME 7 – THE MYSTERIES OF YESOD

Yesod reflects the Virtues of All the Sephiroth – *Part I. Purity :* Purity is a Question of Nourishment – Sorting and Selecting – Purity and the Spiritual Life – Purity in the Three Worlds – The River of Life – Purity and Peace – The Magic of Trusting – Purity and Speech – To Find Purity – Blessed are the Pure in Heart – The Gates of the New Jerusalem – *Part II. Love and Sex* – *Part III. Realization* – The Spring – Fasting – Washing – The Real Baptism – The Angels of the Four Elements.

VOLUME 10 – THE SPLENDOUR OF TIPHARETH

1. Surya-yoga - The Sun, Centre of our Universe – 2. Obtaining Etheric Elements from the Sun - When We Gaze at the Sun Our Soul Begins to Resemble it – 3. Our Higher Self Dwells in the Sun – 4. The Creator Sows Seeds in Us and the Sun Makes Them Grow - The Sun Reflects the Blessed Trinity – 5. Every Creature Has a Home - The Seven Beads of the Rosary – 6. The Master and the Seven-bead Rosary - Every Creature Needs to Own and Protect its Dwelling Place - The Aura – 7. The Heliocentric Point

VOLUME 26 — A NEW DAWN:
Society and Politics in the Light of Initiatic Science — Part II

1. Forms and Principles — 2. The Religion of Christ — 3. The Idea of a Pan-World — 4. The Cosmic Body — 5. The Kingdom of God and His Righteousness — 6. The New Jerusalem.

(A new edition of this volume will be published shortly.)

VOLUME 29 — ON THE ART OF TEACHING
from the Initiatic Point of View

1. Spiritual Work — 2. On Responsibility — 3. On Building the New Life — 4. On the Living Knowledge — 5. On Perfection — 6. On the Reality of the Invisible World — 7. On Participation in the Work of the Universal White Brotherhood.

VOLUME 30 — LIFE AND WORK IN AN INITIATIC SCHOOL
Training for the Divine — Part I

1. The International Day of the Sun — 2. The Bonfin — 3. Training for the Divine — 4. Hrani-Yoga and Surya-Yoga — 5. The Spirit of the Teaching — 6. Matter and Light — 7. Purity and Light — 8. The Meaning of Initiation.

VOLUME 32 — THE FRUITS OF THE TREE OF LIFE
The Cabbalistic Tradition

1. How to Approach the Study of the Cabbalah — 2. The Number Ten and the Ten Sephiroth — 3. Structure and Symbols of the Tree of Life — 4. The Tetragrammaton and the Seventy-Two Planetary Spirits — 5. The Creation of the World and the Theory of Emanation — 6. The Fall and Redemption of Man — 7. The Four Elements — 8. Evening Vigils Round the Fire : I. The Power of Fire — II. Fire and the Sun — III. The Fire of Sacrifice — 9. Water and Fire — 10. A Bowl of Water — 11. The Living Logos : I. The Alphabet and the Twenty-Two Elements of the Logos — II. The Universal Language of the Logos — III. The Power of the Logos — 12. The Esoteric Church of Saint John — 13 Binah, the Realm of Stability — 14. The Human Spirit is Above Fate — 15. Death and the Life Beyond — 16. Human and Cosmic Respiration — 17. The Cardinal Feasts — 18. The Moon and its Influence on Man — 19. The Glorified Souls — 20. The Land of the Living — 21. A Magic Wand — 22. Nature Spirits — 23. Objects are Receptacles of Life — 24. The Holy Grail — 25. Building the Inner Sanctuary.

By the same author:
(translated from the French)

By the same author:
(translated from the French)

Brochures:

301 – The New Year
302 – Meditation
303 – Respiration
304 – Death and the Life Beyond

Daily Meditations:

A thought for each day of the year

Cassette:

KC2510A – The Laws of Reincarnation

Editor-Distributor
Editions PROSVETA S.A. – B.P. 12 – 83601 Fréjus Cedex (France)

Distributors

AUSTRALIA
QUEST, 484 Kent Street
2000 Sydney
AUSTRIA
MANDALA
Magister-Eduard-Angerer-Weg 72
A-6380 St. Johann (Tirol)
BELGIUM
PROSVETA BENELUX
Liersesteenweg 154 B-2547 Lint
N.V. MAKLU Somersstraat 13-15
B-2000 Antwerpen
VANDER S.A.
Av. des Volontaires 321
B-1150 Bruxelles
BRAZIL
NOBEL SA
Rua da Balsa, 559
CEP 02910 - São Paulo, SP
BULGARIA
SVETOGLED
Bd Saborny 16 A appt 11
9000 Varna
CANADA
PROSVETA Inc.
1565 Montée Masson
Duvernay est, Laval, Que. H7E 4P2
COLUMBIA
PROSVETA
Avenida 46 n° 19 – 14 (Palermo)
Santafé de Bogotá
CYPRUS
THE SOLAR CIVILISATION BOOKSHOP
PO Box 4947
Nicosie
GERMANY
PROSVETA DEUTSCHLAND
Gemmiweg 4
72355 Schömberg
EDIS GmbH, Daimlerstr.5
D - 8029 Sauerlach
GREAT BRITAIN
PROSVETA
The Doves Nest,
Duddleswell, Uckfield,
East Sussex TN22 3JJ
GREECE
EDITIONS PROSVETA
J. VAMVACAS
Rue El. Venizelou 4
18531 – Piräus
HOLLAND
STICHTING
PROSVETA NEDERLAND
Zeestraat 50
2042 LC Zandvoort

HONG KONG
SWINDON BOOK CO LTD.
246 Deck 2, Ocean Terminal
Harbour City
Tsimshatsui, Kowloon
IRELAND
PROSVETA IRL.
84 Irishtown – Clonmel
ITALY
PROSVETA Coop.
Casella Postale
06060 Moiano (PG)
LUXEMBOURG
PROSVETA BENELUX
Liersesteenweg 154, B-2547 Lint
MEXICO
COLOFON S.A.
Pitagora 1143
Colonia del Valle
03 100 Mexico, D.F.
NEW ZEALAND
PSYCHIC BOOKS
P.O. Box 87-151
Meadowbank Auckland 5
NORWAY
PROSVETA NORDEN
Postboks 5101
1501 Moss
PORTUGAL
PUBLICAÇÕES
EUROPA-AMERICA Ltd
Est Lisboa-Sintra KM 14
2726 Mem Martins Codex
ROMANIA
ANTAR
Str. N. Constantinescu 10
Bloc 16A - sc A - Apt. 9
Sector 1 - 71253 Bucarest
SPAIN
ASOCIACIÓN PROSVETA ESPAÑOLA
C/ Ausias March n° 23 Ático
SP-08010 Barcelona
SWITZERLAND
PROSVETA
Société Coopérative
CH - 1808 Les Monts-de-Corsier
UNITED STATES
PROSVETA U.S.A.
P.O. Box 49614
Los Angeles, California 90049
VENEZUELA
J.P. Leroy
Apartado 51 745
Sabana Grande
1050 A – Caracas

PRINTED IN FRANCE IN DECEMBER 1995
EDITIONS PROSVETA, Z.I. DU CAPITOU
B.P.12 – 83601 FRÉJUS
FRANCE

– N° d'impression : 2285 –
Dépôt légal : Décembre 1995
Printed in France